GOD'S RICH PATTERN

*Meditations for when our
faith is shaken*

———◆———

Dr Lin Berwick MBE

Dedication
To those of us who are struggling on our
personal spiritual journey . . .

This book endeavours to recognize that struggle
and come to terms with it. We don't always know the
path that God is leading us down, yet we must be open
to seeing how our lives can be enriched by his pattern,
which is woven through everything that we do.

First published in Great Britain in 2012

Society for Promoting Christian Knowledge
36 Causton Street
London SW1P 4ST
www.spckpublishing.co.uk

British Library Cataloguing-in-Publication Data
A catalogue record for this book is available from the British Library

ISBN 978–0–281–06709–1
eBook ISBN 978–0–281–06710–7

Typeset by Graphicraft Ltd, Hong Kong
Printed in Great Britain by Ashford Colour Press
Subsequently digitally printed in Great Britain

Produced on paper from sustainable forests

Contents

Contents

1

God's rich pattern

I write this book from the starting point of having experienced a spiritual breakdown. I'm a fully accredited Methodist Local Preacher with almost fourteen years experience of preaching. By some people's standards that might be classed as minimal, but my calling came out of a very real personal struggle. Right from the age of four years old, daily prayer and scriptural reading were part of my very existence. God and Jesus were my friends. They were as natural to me as breathing.

The certainty was that, whatever was happening in my life, God and Christ were at my shoulder. They were my rock, the foundation on which my life was built, the very bricks and cornerstone of every aspect of my life. I was brain damaged at birth, which resulted in cerebral palsy; I subsequently had surgery (a painful hamstring transplant on both my legs), lost my sight at fifteen years old, which culminated in the removal of both eyes, then had an extremely painful back operation – yet, through all these experiences God was there. In fact, it was after the back surgery in 1978, when I had a near-death experience, that I was given the assurance that God was very much with me. God told me that I wasn't going to die. He had special work for me to do. That special work was heeding the call to preach, and also setting up a charity, The Lin Berwick Trust, with my husband Ralph, to provide holiday accommodation for people with disability, their families and carers.

When I first met Ralph he was a self-confessed atheist. Four years on from our marriage he committed his life to Christ, and became a member of the Methodist Church. I never pushed religion down his throat, and I hope I never spoke in a browbeating way to him about faith. I tried to make him feel a part of the family of Christ by loving him, and those around me, into the kingdom of God, not so much by what I said but by what I did. My philosophy on life is that you can create your own little piece of heaven where you are, or your own little piece of hell. My husband's view, when he realized that God was becoming part of his own existence, was that he didn't want to be on the edge of things. He stood with me at the door of the church, where I believe your ministry is as much about what you do there, and how you respond to people, as what you say from the pulpit.

For many, the human contact with the preacher at the door of the church may be the only sense of a 'spiritual hug' that they have in the course of any one week. I can remember an elderly lady, who was not very popular with those around her as she was argumentative and difficult to get along with. She told me that she had started dancing classes because she was desperate for human touch and contact. I picked up on her loneliness and realized, from the way she responded to me, that it was touch that she needed. She was quite perceptive over my blindness and made sure that she maintained human contact with me. People watched this interaction between us and said how surprised they were that I had such a good response from her. Perhaps it was because I picked up on her need using my 'inner-vision' and sense of perception, which is so greatly needed in difficult circumstances.

My husband Ralph meant the world to me. I never thought I would marry. In fact, I never thought anyone would be mad enough to take me on. But Ralph saw through the disability, the wheelchair and the ramifications of living with a lifetime of caring. He saw the person within, the person beyond the chair. This was a unique and very special gift, and something I'll always treasure him for. When we married, my life took off.

For the first six years it was the most flowering and blossoming experience that I had ever encountered. I had lived a very sheltered life up until that point, but Ralph expanded my life and made me blissfully happy. Then tragedy struck.

I should have been able to call on my faith. I should have had the strength of other Christians to support me. I should have realized that, however dark the valley, I would come out on the other side. After all, I had been in many dark valleys during my lifetime, and I had had the absolute assurance and certainty that I would get through. I would be strengthened by the experience and hopefully not let it make me bitter and twisted, but find the positives out of the negatives and be strengthened by them in such a way that I would be able to be strong for others. However, it didn't work in this case. I was completely and utterly floored by the experience. I had a feeling of being absolutely numb inside. Physically cold, totally turned off. Living my life, as hard as it was – in fact during that time it couldn't have got any harder – limping, metaphorically, through the day, praying for the night-time when I would sleep (sleep was rare) and longing not to wake up.

Looking back, I was in a very deep depression. Tranquillizers were not the answer. They were only a sticking plaster. What I needed was physical support and finance, and at that period of my life they were conspicuous by their absence. I should have been able to turn to God for solace, even if I poured out my anguish rather like Job. This experience left me spiritually dead. Hadn't I already had enough knock-out punches in my life? I couldn't even call out to God, let alone know his presence. As for reading his Scripture, it was, and still largely is, impossible. Whereas in the past the Scriptures came alive when I read my Bible, as I found myself at the Sea of Galilee, or in the Garden of Gethsemane, or present at the Last Supper, now it was just words on a page that seemed so trite. The assurances that God offered were not aspects of expressions of love, or total assurance of the rock, they were just lifeless.

As a preacher, I'm not proud of the admission of these feelings, but I'm sure there are many of you out there who have gone through a similar experience but perhaps can't admit it. It takes terrific courage for me to write on a page that the words of Scripture mean nothing.

At this moment, I've no idea whether that feeling will change. This Easter I had my first sensation, in five years, of wanting to go to church. Sadly, circumstances prevented it and I began to think that this was perhaps my own personal penance, for I couldn't just pick God up when I wanted to, and put him down again. Perhaps the starting of this book is an expression of my owning that God is still there.

The strange thing is, that through all my struggle I've been able to maintain prayer for others and do Christian healing by the laying on of hands and by prayer. Yet I haven't been able to pray for myself. Ministers of the church were a very rare breed of people during this period. When they did appear their prayer was very platitudinal, seeming to have little relevance to what I was feeling inside. Long-term illness is not something that the church does well. Normally, people rally round for a few weeks and then expect everything to come out 'all right'. The people who share their life with you know it's going to be a long haul, but they are there because they want to be there. When it is a spiritual long haul and someone is having a spiritual breakdown it's a bit like the situation of a bereavement. Members of the church don't know what to say, and so often they do not know what to do either. Practical help can be so much more important than glib words.

This book will endeavour, and it can only be endeavour, to empathize with you. I can never put myself in your position. I can never experience your particular circumstances, but through my own struggle I can understand where you might be coming from. I can try to address your anger, fears, anguish, pain and suffering, in a way that gets alongside you, and meets you where you are, and not where you are expected to be. I come from a background of psychotherapeutic counselling, where the silence between counsellor and client can sometimes be so thickly felt that it creates an atmosphere all of its own in the room. Breaking that silence can be very destructive on the one hand, yet therapeutic on the other. The art of counselling is to know what is appropriate and when it is right to do it. Sometimes the silence can be very healing. It is as though you are holding the person's hand. Even though you aren't physically touching them.

I hope that through what I write on these pages I'll be holding your hand, and that together we'll come through and reach the other side.

A thought

Don't try to make things 'all come right'. Just accept that you are where you are at this God-given moment. Sometimes it's necessary just to allow yourself to be, to find that serenity and peace within yourself.

A prayer

Lord, when we cannot feel your presence, don't even want to acknowledge your existence because we hurt so much, help us to find those people around us who can hold us in this difficult situation. Lord, it's so hard to find yourself in a spiritual desert, when nothing has meaning any more. Sometimes, when people talk about the way you are there carrying them, like a footprint that they see in the sand, it so often doesn't feel that you are. When we can't feel that you are there, please, Lord, be there. Give people the courage not to fill the void with words, but allow the space and quietness to grow. So that the person who is hurting may find inner peace and solitude, and thereby eventually find you again. Help us to see, when things happen to us that we don't necessarily understand, that this is part of your rich pattern, and the picture and meaning will reveal itself in the end.

concrete and rock boulders. I used to ride my trike around the park, and occasionally sit on the grass. It wasn't uncommon for me to have as many as twenty-six children sitting on the ground in front of me, asking me to tell them about the stories in the Bible. Their ridicule had turned to interest. Was I being prepared for what was to come many years later? I don't know. But it certainly made me used to voice projection and not being afraid to speak in public!

Again, what might appear to the reader as exceptional for a child of eight or nine years old appeared to me to be perfectly normal. My mother had taken me to a healer, and we were part of a prayer circle that took place at eight o'clock every evening. The prayer circle united us with many hundreds of people, who would be praying for healing and help with difficulties of one kind or another, for certain individuals. I realized the power of togetherness, the power of being united in one common cause, namely the love of Christ. I was always mystified by the healing miracles within the Bible, and through those miracles realized the power of human touch, which to my mind is vitally important. Without good touch you cannot have a good relationship. In my opinion there must be human contact and human interaction. You might say: 'Well, you don't have good touch when it comes to your love for Christ – you are not able to reach out and touch him.' Not in a real, physical sense, that is true. But I was touched emotionally; touched in my heart and mind, reaching out in every sense of the word to a life that was rich and full, and not caught up by worldly, materialistic standards – a life that was governed by Christian principles, which told me that whatever happened God would be there for me. Sometimes, due to medical procedures, I found this hard to believe. If God was in this level of pain and fear, where was he? But the mere fact that I could learn to cope with things, sometimes just five minutes at a time, was enough, for there was no point in thinking of the 'big picture', as that might never happen. Five minutes at a time would mean that I might get through the day, and I certainly did, because as I write this I'm in my sixtieth year. A miracle in itself.

What happens then when your rock is shattered? As I thought about this I had an image of an implosion, or an earthquake, because rocks that have been there for a long time don't normally shatter. But when a disaster strikes, even on the level of a small human one by global standards, it feels like an earthquake and a massive explosion of everything that you hold dear. Nothing seems tangible anymore. All the things that you took for granted suddenly diminish. There is nothing to hold on to, and your world and life seem meaningless. So, what can you do? All you can do is stay with it, and hold on to the pieces of your life that you can still acknowledge. In my case, it was praying for others.

Having a ministry of healing, I know that in weakness there can also be wholeness. In weakness there is also strength, as we saw through Christ's crucifixion. In weakness there can also be a resurrection, a sense of new beginnings and hope. But when things are dark, all you can do is hang on in there, knowing that after a time you will come out on the other side, although it doesn't seem like that when you are immersed in what is happening to you, and you feel totally traumatized by the event. Remember, just five minutes at a time. Even a day, when you are up against it, can seem far too long. When I suffered great pain during surgery, I dealt with it in five-minute chunks, hoping that the next day wouldn't be so bad. It is so difficult when day after day you are immersed in a particular tragedy, or crisis of faith, and it doesn't seem to get any better. In my case, my crisis of faith, as I write this, is something of a thirteen-year period.

I was not capable of praying for me. The only words I could get out were 'Why, Lord? Why did this have to happen? Why did you take away the most precious thing in my life, leaving me a total void?' There have been times when I screamed it at the wall and shouted these words with my head raised to heaven, not knowing where the help would come from. But amazingly, I'm still here and I'm writing this text, and my solid piece of mountainous rock may now only be a small boulder, but it's still there, and to me that's most important.

A thought

When familiar things that we hold dear are taken from us, or shattered due to an event, it is hard to believe that we will ever recover. But time is a great healer and this is not a cliché. Time will heal. Sometimes it is important to clear away the dead wood before we can rebuild. We have to hold on to the things in our life that give us stability and continuity; then reshape them like the potter and the clay to make a totally new and transformed object. In this case, the object is our life and our fundamental belief and knowledge of the love of Christ. It's difficult at times to believe. But in all aspects of faith it is about trust in the things we cannot see, rather than the things we can. Values and concepts, not materialism, are what matters. The love expressed by one human being to another in genuine friendship and concern becomes our rock when our faith deserts us. The faith is still there, but we can't always see it, or don't always want to see it.

A prayer

Lord, continue to be our rock when all else fails. Continue to be our strength, our firm foundation. Bring the people that we need to help and support us through this dark day. Give us the resolve to keep going, even when we feel like giving up. Help us to find spiritual renewal, mental peace, serenity of spirit, wholeness of mind, even in the darkest days.

3

Steps of faith

At eleven years old I was given the opportunity of a pioneering surgical procedure, which would, it was hoped, enable me to walk. The medical team told me that it would be a very painful procedure, and that if I decided to take the opportunity I would have to be very brave. This is hard for a small child to take on board. It was to be a hamstring transplant operation on both my legs. How could I pass up the opportunity of learning to walk? It would be an incredible challenge, yet would give me the sense of dignity and normality that I longed for. No one wants to be crawling on hands and knees in their teenage years, if it can possibly be avoided. So I went into hospital in February 1962. I can remember that morning as though it were yesterday. Snow was falling in huge flakes, covering the ground quickly in a white blanket. Somehow it seemed very poignant looking out of the lounge window with my two brothers, one on either side of me. All of us forcing back the tears – mine of fear, wondering if I would ever see my home again. At this point in my life I had never been separated from my mother. The prospect of that alone was scary.

I can remember the long walk in my father's arms as we trundled down the hospital corridors. In those days, the smell of pine, Dettol and floor polish was very evident. No neat decoration on the hospital walls, just green tiles that were to be my visual existence for eleven weeks and four days. Remember what I said about five minutes at a time? Well, I learnt this philosophy extremely quickly after this operation, because it was one of the most agonizingly painful experiences I have ever encountered. To complete the surgery on both legs, together with manipulation (under anaesthetic, because it would be so painful), I had three trips to the operating theatre in a fortnight. This was terrifying and I will never forget that feeling as the gas mask was placed over my face. Perhaps that is why I am claustrophobic now when things are put over my head. My mind always goes back to that moment and I can smell the ether.

Eleven weeks and four days in hospital with the most intense pain was bad enough. But I had a total of six months in plaster from toes to thighs, with a wooden bar between my knees to keep my legs separated during the night. Sleeping was horrendously difficult. When it came to the physiotherapy, when the plaster was cut, and they had to bend the knees for the first time without anaesthetic, I lashed out, hit the physio and screamed violently. If God was there – where was he? This was my crucifixion, my Calvary. But if I was able to walk at the end of it that would be my resurrection.

One year on from the start of the surgery, I took my first steps. Just four. But they were my giant leap for mankind. All of my family members were there in the lounge of my home. We ended up in a heap, hugging each other. What joy – twelve years of pain and struggle, but I'd made it. The world was my oyster. I would be able to walk, albeit slowly and painfully on tripod sticks. What a victory.

All the efforts of my parents were coming to glorious fruition. It had been worth all the sacrifices that they had had to make. My parents' life, as a couple, had been put on hold while Mum chased me backwards and forwards to hospitals three times a week for physiotherapy, as well as other hospital appointments. Through my efforts they had their reward, and it was a wonderful moment for us all. I cannot begin to express what it's like suddenly to have the sensation of standing on your own, albeit with sticks to support you, and to realize that you can move independently and make your own decisions as to where you will go and what you want to do, rather than being reliant on others.

My world would now take off. This was a great confidence booster. But tragedy was to strike yet again, taking away what confidence I had. This victory was not without cost, for the physical pain that I endured during the surgery caused me to have a mental breakdown. I spent the next two and a half years on tranquillizers. I used to feel terribly fearful when my mother left me, and I couldn't wait for her to return. Whether the breakdown was due to the pain, or all the anaesthetic, I guess we will never know. This new-found situation meant the security of my world had suddenly been taken away, and through my own particular vulnerability I then had to rebuild things again, which wasn't easy. Nothing we do in life is without cost, but sometimes you have to go through trauma to find success.

A thought

When we are consumed by fear we have to put our trust in the things that we hold dear. That may be particular people. If they are not there we have to be reliant on something at a higher level. If this is God, what a privilege. This story is living proof that out of trauma can come joy. Yet nothing is without a price. The price in this case was pain, suffering and isolation. Time did heal, but healing cannot be rushed.

A prayer

Lord, there will be many people suffering physical pain and emotional anguish for one reason or another. Help them through the chaos of pain and suffering to know that you are there, to feel your hand upon them, strengthening, guiding and blessing. Help those people not to be traumatized by the experience that they are facing. Help them to be outward looking, willing to face the future, reaching out to whatever opportunity comes their way. Sometimes, Lord, the pain people experience is emotional pain. This is nonetheless real. It causes as much anguish as physical pain, sometimes more. Help them to find ways of dealing with the emotional anguish, of reconciling it to themselves, of learning, through the anguish, ways in which they can grow and be strong to face the rest of their lives.

4

A change to my world

———•◦•———

I had learnt to walk at the age of thirteen, and I started to enjoy the freedom of movement. I had been partially sighted all my life due to oxygen damage of the eyes at birth. I had gone to an ophthalmic hospital for my usual check-up. The doctor seemed to take an incredibly long time to examine my right eye.

'Your little girl is very brave,' the doctor said to my mum.

'Yes, she's a fighter,' was Mum's response.

'And she's going to need a whole lot more courage too,' he said.

Alarm bells started ringing in my head. Especially when I heard the words 'We'll have to admit her.' Examinations under anaesthetic showed that I had a detached retina. Doctors told me that I would be totally blind within three months. I didn't take it in at first, because I had a thumping headache from the examinations. I suppose I was numbed by this statement. After all, what did it really mean and what was my life going to be like? I'd had two years of freedom and movement, and now at fifteen years old, with deteriorating vision, I was afraid to move. This realization was quite shocking. Further examinations took place and, as I waited to go down to the operating theatre yet again, I started to pray.

'Please Lord, let it all come right,' I prayed. 'Let the original diagnosis be wrong.' I lay in my hospital bed shaking with fear, praying through the night. And then the words 'Take this cup away from me' came into my head. Of course, at that time, I would have given anything for the cup to be taken away. But on reflection, I thought, 'Who am I to feel that I should not have this problem over and above anyone else? Why me? should also be Why not me?' Later that night I had a sudden calm come over me as the words 'Not my will but thine be done' also sank into my brain. I knew that whatever happened in that operating theatre I would be all right. Sadly, there was nothing that could be done for my sight. As I was already blind in my left eye, total blindness would occur.

I should have been terrified; and I was terrified of waking up each morning and seeing the further gradual deterioration. But when the sight finally failed I had an inner peace. Blindness cuts you off from worldly perception. You are not caught up by first impression. You no longer take people on face value, but you get to know them for who they are and what they are. This is a very great privilege, because it teaches you that worldly values count for very little, and the things that we hold dear don't really matter.

Now I really was in the dark, in more ways than one. Blindness, most of all, teaches you patience because it can be incredibly frustrating, but it also teaches you resilience. I say to people that going blind was the best thing that ever happened to me, in terms of getting a decent education and realizing that I had a brain. I would now get the chance to be educated as a blind person.

A thought

All of us have our dark valley from time to time. We all feel that we are floundering in the dark, tripping over obstacles in our life. What we need is someone to take us by the hand and guide us out into the open again. It is necessary for all of us to immerse ourselves in the experience that we are faced with; to learn how to deal with the changes, especially the emotional changes, before we can adequately face the rest of the world. So, although I have been speaking about blindness, it is a metaphor for life in general.

A prayer

Lord, when we enter our own particular dark valley, be with us. Be that small still voice of calm in the darkness. Be our guiding hand to help us when we stumble. Take hold of us, reassure us, strengthen us to go forward, unfalteringly, into the light. Help us to value ourselves and not apologize for being who we are, with all our limitations. But help us to face the world around us with pride.

5

Coming out of the darkness

Blindness makes you draw on inner resources and get in touch with the world around you in a different way. Sound is all important. Music can be a wonderful comforter, enabling one to get on a higher spiritual plane. My first introduction to classical music was a recording of Beethoven's Pastoral Symphony No. 6. What an introduction that proved to be, especially as Beethoven was critically deaf when he created the Pastoral Symphony. Yet it is colour in sound, in the most incredible way. Listening to the 'By the Brook' movement, one can imagine walking by the water. The depiction of the storm really gives you a feeling of the weather closing in and dark clouds overhead. That could be said of my life at this point. Dark clouds overhead; so many changes, so many new experiences to come to terms with. Learning Braille was no easy task, especially when the first Braille book that I was trying to read had dots that had almost gone to powder, because it was so old. The frustration was incredible, yet getting in touch with the world around one was also exhilarating. Mastering Braille was the first major challenge. Learning to cope with one's food and not being afraid to move were yet more challenges.

What I dealt with at this point was so crucial for the rest of my life. Taking hold of experiences, grasping them with both hands and making the most of every God-given moment. Remember that 'five minutes at a time'? Well, it still held true. Life was a series of hurdles that had to be surmounted and overcome. The victories were often tiny, but well won. Music was my salvation. It transported me into another world: a world that was free of stress. The music was expressive, depicting all kinds of mood, enabling me to get in touch with myself, and thereby gathering strength for what was to come.

A thought

There will be many storms and dark clouds in our lives. Sometimes situations are so bleak that we cannot see our way out of them. All we can do is ride the storm. We must keep in touch with our world, even though it is very difficult, and search for that something which brings meaning and wholeness.

A prayer

Lord, when times are hard help us to get in touch with the parts of ourselves that can transcend the difficulties we are facing. Help us to appreciate the finer things in our world – the artistry of a beautiful picture, the joy of wonderfully expressive music. Lord, it is always amazing when we hear a beautiful piece of music and think of the composer putting notes on a page, which convert to such wonderful sound. Help us all to get in touch with our creative side and be aware of the spirituality around us.

6

A window on the world

————•••————

The joy of discovering that I had a brain soaking up English literature, music and choral singing was fantastic. I'd had, until blindness struck, only a very basic education. It was really only occupation of the mind, rather than learning life skills. Now, at my school for the blind, teachers realized that I had something between my ears other than sawdust. And what joy, as I was pushed by the teachers beyond what I felt was my limit. Discovering all kinds of literature and being put in for O levels. No mean achievement when I had only just gone blind. I was also entered for Grades III and IV flute exam, with the Royal Academy of Music. The discipline of playing music correctly, getting as conversant with it as it was possible to be, and understanding music theory (which for me by and large was anathema), getting to grips with it and winning was marvellous.

I was on my way, succeeding and not apologizing for being in this world; accepting that whatever the difficulties I had a right to be here. How many of us, when we struggle through life, feel that we don't belong. With multi-disability, body image was something of a problem. Would I be taken seriously by the great public out there? It was hard to tell. I could only press on regardless, trying to make my way and make a difference – not least of all in the attitude of one person to another. I have always said that one person's attitude towards a person's disability today might be another person's response to that same person tomorrow. Because none of us knows, from minute to minute, how our life can suddenly change. We all have to be open to the challenge of change, however difficult.

In so many incidents throughout my life I was written off as one of society's 'non-achievers'. Now I was achieving, albeit slowly. I could not be pushed to one side, or stuck in a corner out of the way. Life was there for the taking – and I was going to grasp it. I decided to train as a switchboard operator upon leaving school. After passing my course at the RNIB Commercial Training College, I started to look for work. It felt as though I would never be taken seriously. It would be difficult for a person with multiple disability to gain employment over someone who was able-bodied. I had to be so good at what I did, so skilled, that I stood out from the rest. I had the most enormous personal mission, which was to prove that I was as good as anybody else, and that I could happily play my part as a member of the workforce.

Being a switchboard operator is a very specialized job. You are the window of the company that you serve. You are the first representative that the caller hears. First impressions of the voice do count. Smiling as you answer the telephone makes a huge difference to the tone of the voice. Regular callers to the bank where I worked became my friends. I had a wealth of acquaintances, people of varying interests from all different walks of life. Yet another window had opened on that big wide world out there. I was motoring, things were really going to happen. I would just have to wait and see.

A thought

Life can be full of frightening challenges. We have to be prepared to accept them and realize that we may only get one chance – one bite of a very delicious cherry, which, if we fail to take it, may alter the course of our life forever. Being terrified to accept challenges can make us stultified, can make us dull in our mental responses. Someone who is eager to accept challenges is usually mentally bright and alert. Education with all its challenges can be like this. If we grasp opportunities we can grow. But if we let the worry of daily life drag us down, we will be one of life's non-achievers. No success in education, or employment, ever comes easily. It is hard fought and hard won.

Take up the challenge. Even in a dark moment. Be brave and bold and follow your star.

A prayer

Lord, when we are inhibited by fear, the fear of failure because we assume that we are not up to the challenges that you present us with, help us to relish in the power of learning. Help us to have inquisitive minds. Help us to stick to the task tenaciously, relentlessly, and rejoice in our success. But be there for us if we fail. Help us to really value the opportunities that we have been given, and make something of each of your God-given days.

7

Taking up the challenge

———•◆•———

I had spent much of my childhood in the company of my parents, who were working for spastic children (now better known as people with cerebral palsy). Their aim, as one of the first parent groups, later to be known as SCOPE, was initially to raise money for a treatment centre. Later, because more physiotherapy was offered on the NHS, they changed the focus of their ambition to providing a social centre where people with disabilities could meet on a regular basis.

Within that social centre I realized that there was precious little being done for young adolescents and people in their twenties and thirties. We did not want the kind of entertainment that only paid lip service to us, and in fact treated us as though we were all in our dotage. We wanted to be out there, experiencing life the same as anyone else – going to theatres, restaurants and places of interest. Because I raised this issue at many meetings of the organization, I was asked to form a social club for young people with cerebral palsy. However, I was determined to put a different slant on the matter. I wanted my organization to be more inclusive, to be not only for people with cerebral palsy, but with all different disabilities. Furthermore, I wanted the able-bodied to be a part of that group, befriending those with disability.

There was much opposition to this idea, but when I get a bee in my bonnet I am quite tenacious. Eventually, I persuaded the committee to go along with it, and in 1969 I was given a grant of £50 which, certainly by today's standard, was derisory. I had to start somewhere. I quickly realized that my idea would never truly get off the ground unless we had our own transport. To begin with we were using anything that had four wheels and an engine to ferry people to and from venues. But I managed to persuade people that to raise funds for our own hydraulic tailgate ambulance would be the best solution.

I involved the local Rotary clubs, Worshipful Companies in the City, colleagues at the bank where I worked, and the bank's press office, who were very keen to help my endeavours. Eventually we took delivery of our first vehicle. This was the passport to getting many people with disability out and about. Some were in their twenties and thirties, yet they had never been to a restaurant, or had the experience of going to a West End cinema or theatre. It was difficult raising funds for such events, yet I was able to capture the imagination of so many who helped with fundraising, and take people with disability out of the medical model in which they frequently found themselves, and put them on a level playing field with their able-bodied peers. This was challenging, exciting and rewarding.

I had no idea where it would take me but I just let the spirit lead. The club, eventually known as the Disabled Fellowship Club of East London (now disbanded), was thriving. Membership was growing as people realized that this was an organization worth belonging to. There was only one thing for it – raise funds for a second vehicle, and I was very much in the media spotlight. There always seemed to be articles in the paper about me, and I was frequently on Capital Radio with the presenters Joan Shenton and Tommy Vance. However, I needed a team of drivers. It was no good having the vehicles if they were standing still. So the local policemen at several Essex police stations formed a rota of drivers to help me with this project. They were skilled in first aid, and, more importantly, they had people skills and were great with those who were profoundly disabled.

In those days the authorities were not so hot on health and safety and manual handling; as long as you could offer the assistance that someone needed, and were willing to do so, that was fine. Our members thrived on this socialization. It became the highlight of their week. I do not think I had ever gone out quite so much myself.

So in trying to help others, I was helping myself, improving my own social interaction and gaining confidence. There was a purpose to my own disability because I was able to recognize the needs of others – had I not sat alongside them, and shared in their difficulties, I would never have gained such knowledge and understanding.

A thought

In everything that we do in life there is a purpose, although we may not be able to see it at the time. We just have to be open to whatever challenges present themselves. Each challenge is a learning curve by which we grow. There is no shame in trying something and failing. The shame is never trying at all.

A prayer

Lord, help us not to be fearful when challenges present themselves. Help us to be open-minded enough to let the spirit lead. Help us to understand that in you all things are possible. When opportunities open themselves to us, help us to be brave and bold enough to take them.

8

A new way of communicating

The media attention that I have just mentioned took me to places of which I would never have dreamt. A friend, who had multiple sclerosis, ran a regional branch of the Muriel Braddick Foundation. This provided taped music, Christian thought and personalized interviews, for people who were confined to their home or were in hospital, and in some cases very seriously ill, such as in a coma.

I contacted Muriel, who was a member of the Salvation Army, to ask for a tape for a friend. At that point I did not mention my own disability. Due to the fact that I had been involved with so many broadcasts and newspaper feature articles, I became fascinated with the world of the media in general, and how broadcasting could be a great source of outreach for people with disability. I offered to help Muriel expand her tape interview service, and I became the Public Relations Officer for the Foundation. In the six and a half years that I worked for the Foundation, I set up many interviews that could be used in all kinds of situations. I can remember one young man, who was profoundly disabled in hospital, who wanted a message from the BBC *Test Match Special* Team. I contacted Brian Johnston, then the senior member of the team, and he very kindly made a recording with all the people in the commentary box. The young man absolutely loved this, and it gave him a sense of purpose and a will to go on.

This was the amazing sense of outreach that the Foundation had towards its people. We never quite knew how folk would respond, but it was wonderful when our goodwill messages and music bought so much happiness to others. Could there be something here that would help me to develop my skills within the media? I had no idea but I was sure I would be led to the answer in due course.

A thought

It is hard to get to grips with just how powerful the spoken word and the impact of music can be. Music speaks all languages and transcends all boundaries. We can never know what will touch someone's heart and mind. Mostly, it is because someone has shown that they care and reached out to another human being. And in this day of impersonal communication through the internet, where so many, although they are in touch with the world, are in isolation, it is even more important to remember the power of the human voice.

A prayer

Lord, when we are experiencing feelings of fear, desolation and isolation, when we feel desperately alone, help us to be an open channel to you, where we can communicate our feelings however bizarre and off-the-wall they might seem. Help us to know that you will accept the good feelings as well as the bad. That you will not judge us, but help us to come to terms with the difficulties that we find ourselves in. It is not easy, especially when we feel the only person that is to blame is ourself. We know that this does not make our guilt any easier to bear, but we ask that you will accept us, warts and all, and love us through it.

9

Where to now?

The work of a public relations officer took me into many different areas. I became so well known at the BBC that the car park attendants and security staff used to greet me by my name as I came in with my trusty tape recorder. I produced many good interviews that were used by the Foundation. Then I had cause to be an in-patient at Moorfields Eye Hospital, where I had my left eye removed in 1976.

When you have your head heavily bandaged, and you are feeling frightened by what is happening to you, you appreciate the power of the human voice. It was at this point that I realized the potential and the purpose that was being played out, literally before my eyes – or the lack of them.

Some weeks after my surgery, I was asked to go back to the hospital and speak on Moorfields Hospital Radio about my life and the experience of having an eye removed, and also to choose some of my favourite pieces of music. It was a sort of extended version of *Desert Island Discs*. My broadcast was extremely well received. People liked my voice over the airwaves and my choice of music. The radio staff invited me to have my own programme. I jumped at this chance. This was a great thrill to me. I decided to call the programme *Lin Berwick Meets* and this was the start of a five-year relationship between me and the patients. This work was an extension of what I had been doing for the Muriel Braddick Foundation for many years, namely interviewing famous people and getting them to choose favourite pieces of music. This is where I met my good friend Sue MacGregor CBE.

When I contacted her, asking for an interview, I deliberately omitted to tell her of my own disabilities. She was greatly surprised when we met. However, we struck up a firm friendship, which remains to this day. I chose people who I felt had beautiful voices, or very interesting ones, as I knew from my own experience that interesting voices, when you had a thumping headache, with bandages around your head, were very important. One extremely memorable broadcast was with Rolf Harris – two hours of great fun with Rolf in the studio talking about his life and work, and getting me to attempt to play the didgeridoo and the wobble board!

Other contributors were people such as Desmond Wilcox, Esther Rantzen, Googie Withers, Robin Ellis, James Galway, Edward Woodward, Valerie Singleton and many, many more. What fun it all was. But where was it leading? I was growing in confidence, getting used to speaking to many people from different walks of life and not being fearful. What I had to make sure of was that, despite all this, I kept my feet firmly on the ground. Yes, I got a great deal of fun and satisfaction out of what I did, but I never lost sight of who it was really for. If I had done that then it would not have been blessed.

A thought

It is so easy to be carried away by the moment. To be full of what we are doing, forgetting the opportunity that we have been given, and the privilege of following our own particular star. But it is also vitally important that we keep our feet on the ground. When we are successful, climbing the ladder, we must always remember that if we tread on people on our way up, we have to meet them on our way down. It is a wonderful experience to have one's head in the clouds, but it is not always easy to come back down to earth with a bump.

A prayer

Lord, it is such a privilege when we are open to opportunity, when we do that 'blue sky' thinking which comes off. Lord, help us never to forget that you are part of this rich pattern of life. The threads which are carefully woven into the finest tapestry. So often we cannot see the full picture, until close to our life's end. Help us to see that you have been guiding, shaping, communicating and helping us to be fulfilled, enabling us to be richly blessed by the experiences, good and bad, that we are given.

10

A change of direction

Thrilled though I was to have employment in the City of London, I could not see myself remaining as a telephonist of a city bank for ever. As much as I tried to do the work to the very best of my ability, after six years I became bored and thought that I had to stretch my mind a bit more. I started to study psychology. Initially I did this as a part-time course studying in the evenings, but the more my mind was opened by what I read, dealing with the great thinkers of our century from both a psychological point of view and a religious point of view, the more I realized that I could not stand still.

I found this period in my life wonderfully illuminating. Like a flower coming into bloom, discovering my own individuality. Nothing, however, is achieved without cost. The more you get involved intellectually and academically, the more you draw away from your familiar roots, if you come from a working-class background as I did. Your family are not able to reach you. My family could not understand the concept of counselling. Their attitude was that what went on behind your street door was nobody else's business. To share your problems with somebody else would not be helpful, and would in many instances be seen as disloyal to your family and all that it stood for.

This is an attitude that is very hard to break down in the counselling relationship. What my family could never understand was the concept of having personal therapy while you were training as a counsellor. This is an essential prerequisite of any professional counsellor. We have to understand where the client is coming from. We have to know what it is like to be on the opposite side of the room to the counsellor. Understanding the process from the client's point of view. To my family, however, this was complete madness, a waste of time and, more importantly, a waste of money. But for me this was a time of growth, of awareness and an opportunity to get in touch with personal spirituality, as I was training with a Christian organization where spiritual matters were very much in evidence within the work of counselling.

The activities that I have previously spoken of were still running alongside this new-found career. I was stretching myself to the limit – mentally and physically. There were a great many stairs for me to negotiate and I was usually shattered after climbing them. But with every new obstacle that had to be overcome there was a real sense of achievement and challenge. When I look at the part that God's rich pattern has played in all of this, I can see now that my telephone technique and my interview skills stood me in good stead for interviewing counselling clients. I needed to be able to put them at their ease, to be warm, relaxed and friendly, yet businesslike; to give them the space to express good feelings as well as bad, and to realize that within the counselling relationship there is unconditional positive regard and, I truly hope, non-possessive warmth.

For unlike relationships within a family, which can often be too clinging and binding, almost to the point of suffocation, the counselling relationship is one where we allow the person to grow in confidence – discovering themselves, finding solutions by talking through the problem in a quiet and peaceful manner.

My telephone technique helped me tremendously in the counselling relationship when many years later I ran a crisis telephone line for people with disabilities. This was to be one of my forms of employment for some twenty-three years. During that time I answered hundreds of phone calls from distressed people. Many of the calls that I took were repeats, so I came to know the callers exceedingly well. But what a privilege it was to reach out to someone, even though in the case of telephone counselling I might never actually meet them. Through this example you will see how my life is forming a particular pattern of practical help, empathy, support and understanding. It is the most enormous privilege.

A thought

Sometimes when we are stuck doing a job that we may not like we have to focus on the fact that the job may be a means to an end. In my case, being a switchboard operator of a city bank gave me the finance to study in the evening, and to spread my wings emotionally, intellectually and spiritually. If we could see our employment in terms of the means by which we deal with things that we are truly interested in, then I feel we would have a far better attitude towards it. I know it might be said that that may be because I did not have the responsibility of running a home and children, and all the expenditure that brings, but one has to start somewhere. It is important that we are forever open to the opportunities that we are given.

A prayer

Lord, we may not be able to see where our life is going. We may often find ourselves at a crossroads and not know which way to turn. Sometimes we will be influenced by others, who will lead us up the wrong path. Help us to truly focus on the values of life that are really important. Help us to see that each of us has a duty to reach out to another human being in love and friendship. Help us to create our own little piece of heaven where we are, reaching out to those who are having what they feel is their moment of hell.

11

Another interesting twist

Remember how I said that all the things that have happened so far were part of God's rich pattern? Broadcasting was still very much my first love, but I never thought an opportunity would come quite like this one. David Wood, the manager at the bank, came into the switchboard room one day, and asked what I was doing on Wednesday. I had just come back from a session of physiotherapy at St Bartholomew's (Barts) Hospital. I told him I had nothing planned.

'Well, you're coming on a gin sling with me!' he said with a smile in his voice. He did not normally invite me to social events, so I knew there was something more important behind his invitation. He was walking round and round my switchboard room box, rattling the keys in his pocket.

'For God's sake, David, stand still,' I said. 'I can't locate where you are.' His explanation was that the bank was having a PR exercise between England and Australia that would be filmed. He wanted me, as the senior telephonist, to wish everybody down under at our Australian offices a happy Christmas. I was incredulous; what a waste of money.

The day dawned and I had a splitting headache and did not feel very well. My mother said that if I was unwell I had better go back to bed. She would tell Mr Wood that I could not do it. I decided that I would make the effort and crawl out of bed, despite the pain in my head. My mother was insistent on washing my hair at 5.15 in the morning, which I thought was a little odd.

'You wouldn't want your hair sticking up,' she said, 'if you're going to be filmed.' In the late morning a large van pulled up at the side entrance of the bank. Everyone was abuzz, because on the side it read 'Australian News Reel'. Later in the day the bank entrance hall was transformed into a party scene. Christmas trees, lights, food and drink were in abundance. As I went onto the second floor of the bank that afternoon for my usual comfort stop, I had the manager's secretary walking along with me in deep conversation. That had never happened before. Eventually, it was time to close the switchboard and go to the party. I was offered a drink but declined because of the medication I was taking at the time. Then I heard a squeal of delight, and a voice that I recognized.

'It's my pleasure to be able to say to a very remarkable young lady: "Tonight, Lin Berwick, 'This is Your Life'".'

It was Eamonn Andrews of the Thames TV *This is Your Life* programme with his famous big red book.

I was gobsmacked! Everybody around me was cheering, yet I was dumbstruck. So weak in the knees in fact that my father, who appeared from the shadows, had to pick me up and carry me out of the bank. As we went out of the entrance I was aware of large groups of people standing on the pavement and sitting on every available space. They thought they were going to see a famous person. Many had spotted Eamonn with his big red book as he walked into the bank's entrance hall. Instead they got me, carried out and put into the waiting Daimler.

Eamonn was most solicitous, asking me if I was all right.

'I don't know,' I said, 'I feel sick, give me some air!'

The car whisked me off to Thames Television, where I was locked in the Green Room waiting for the make-up people and technicians. I asked to see my mother and was told that was not possible. But I told them that if I did not see my mother I was not going on! She was quickly brought. Now I could see the reason for the posh new outfit and so-called Christmas shopping day that was not. My mother and father were in rehearsals at the television centre, whilst I was at the bank. I decided that I wanted to walk on to the set. This was something worth standing for. Eamonn came into the dressing room and practised guiding me around. He was very good at it. There was a high step up onto the back of the set, for which I had to be lifted.

'Three steps forward, Lin,' Eamonn guided, 'and turn right.'

At that moment it all began, with that very famous familiar theme tune. I was on the set and the programme was being recorded without a break. Thames Television brought many people to the programme, some of which I had not seen for years, others that I had never actually met – like one of my friends in Australia. They contacted a priest who was in the village of Cushpar, Pakistan. He had to drive one hundred miles to get to the nearest telephone. Another friend was flown over from Canada. Afterwards there was a fantastic party to which all the people who had been interviewed, regardless of whether they appeared on the programme, and fifty-two of my work colleagues, were invited.

'Don't worry, it won't be seen by many people,' Eamonn said to me before I went on the set. Afterwards, he told me that the programme would be seen by thirty million. That was in the days when *This is Your Life* was at the height of its popularity. That sort of coverage is something that I just could not get my head around. The programme was screened one week later. I had over a hundred letters from viewers, many of whom had disabled children or relatives. They found the programme inspiring and wanted to congratulate me on my achievements. The reaction of people in the city of London was most strange. If they saw me coming in or out of the bank they just wanted to come up and shake my hand. This could be extremely tricky if I was negotiating a flight of steps with tripod sticks.

But what did all this mean? Again, I had to keep my feet on the ground. It was a way of reaching out to people, especially those who may be despairing about disability – either the person themselves or a parent or loved one. It was the opportunity to show that despite disability life can still go on and be meaningful and purposeful.

Where it would take me, I had no idea. What it showed me was that I was now, for good or ill, something of a public figure in the disability world. This would give me a profile for the work that I was trying to do for people with disability and their families. My mother always said that she hated the publicity that came with my recognition. Secretly I know that despite what she said she loved it, and was deeply proud of that broadcast and everything that it meant.

As for Eamonn Andrews and the researchers, I kept in touch with them. And I am still friendly with the researchers of the programme today. Members of the research team, and sometimes Eamonn, would ring me. They could not tell me who was going to appear, but they said it was someone I would find interesting, so would I like to come? They would send a car, and I would be taken to the studio, watch the programme and go to the party afterwards. I did this on a number of occasions and it was a great thrill to me to keep my links with the programme and have such fun. I kept in contact with Eamonn right up until the week of his death. He used to write all his letters in green ink because he was Irish.

There are many people who feel nervous about meeting someone. They often feel they are going to be rejected, even before a relationship has begun. It all depends on the approach and the sense of openness that we have to those that we meet. If we adopt an attitude of suspicion, or rejection, the friendship is never going to get off the ground. If, however, we see every new encounter as an opportunity for personal growth, or friendship, then we will approach that person with a totally different attitude.

A thought

When our life takes these interesting turns, we have to go with them. We have to try to discover what we can draw from the experience, and turn it into something very positive. Physical disability, or other disabling conditions that are not clearly visible, do not always have a good press. The media is a very candyfloss world, very shallow. The image on the screen has got to be perfect. So when people with disabilities are represented, it sends a clear message to the viewer. Not everyone is perfect. Not everyone can have their imperfections airbrushed out.

A prayer

Lord, the media in all its forms has the power to excite, inspire, thrill, sadden and shock. Lord, we live in a world where the media is instant. No more the slow deliberation of thought, putting together your feelings on paper. Now, the horrors of what others can do can be in our living rooms within an instant. The immediacy is shocking, but the media can also be a powerful tool to create change. Lord, we live in a world where abnormal perfection is the order of the day. Not all of us can have our imperfections erased. We have to accept there are certain things that we can't change. Help us, Lord, to love ourselves and the imperfections of others. Help us to be discerning of what we watch on television, hear on the radio, read in a magazine, or look at over the internet. For good rather than for ill, let the media be a powerful tool and source of creative influence within all of us.

12

Trials and tribulations

After all the excitement, it was down to earth with a bang. As I stated earlier, I had my left eye removed in 1976. Two years later my right eye (the one I had seen out of) started to play up. The pains in my head were tremendous. It was as though I had a migraine every single day. I had been on medication for glaucoma since 1970. Now, my body had started to reject the medication. I had grown painfully thin. Every time I tried to eat anything I felt very sick, and certain foods that I had eaten all my life were now impossible.

One day I started to haemorrhage from my stomach, due to the medication. The drugs were stopped immediately. Within three weeks the pressure in my eye had built up to such an extent that I could not stand the pain any longer. I went back to Moorfields and told them that despite all the painkilling eye drops and other medication, I had had enough. Doctors said that they were waiting for me to make that decision. I thought, 'Why on earth didn't they tell me?' I was hanging on, hoping for a miracle. My father was horrified when he heard that I had told the doctors to get rid of the eye, and he wanted me to have further tests to make sure that nothing could be done. This took the form of infrared photography of the back of the eye, with pictures taken under a bubble of water. It showed that the eye had been crushed, due to the pressure of glaucoma. I went into hospital for its removal.

Within three weeks I was back at work with a temporary shell in the eye socket. People said to me that I was absolutely amazing. They could not understand why I was so cheerful.

They would have, if they had experienced the pain I had been in for the last eight years. To be free of that terrific pain in the head was liberation. It wasn't easy, coming to terms with the fact that I would never be able to see again, despite what advancements medical science might bring. For the first time since I had started to lose my sight thirteen years earlier, I now had to truly confront the issue of total blindness for life.

There is, however, a certain inner peace and serenity that comes with acceptance. When we kick at the traces, hankering for something that we cannot have, it never brings mental peace. People asked me what I was going to do now. My response was that I was going to go back to playing the flute again. Doctors had prevented me from playing due to the pressure of blowing. As soon as I was well enough, I took myself off to a music shop in London and bought a solid silver Yamaha flute. I still have it to this day. It has been my source of delight and frustration for all these years. It gives me tremendous exercise of the lungs, and occupies my mind when I need to take myself out of what is happening for a while. It's also a great source of manual dexterity for my fingers, and helps me to keep my hands in working order.

If we look hard enough, there will be a silver lining in whatever befalls us. Now that I had had the eye removed, and my pain was greatly lessened, I could get down to the serious business of asking my bank for a year off. When they questioned me why I wanted it, I told them I was going to study analytical psychology. Their response was that it had nothing to do with banking, but they would let me do this, and keep my job open so that I had something to go back to when my year's training course had finished.

Many people thought I was stark raving mad. Fancy giving up a secure job, and taking a training opportunity scheme grant, which effectively lost me £65 per week in earnings, to study psychology, when I had no idea where such a subject would take me, or whether I could make a career out of it. Yet, me being me, I had to grasp the opportunity with both hands.

A thought

When disaster strikes, it seems that we will never get out through the other side. Sometimes, however, we have to go through our own personal dark valley, see what we can learn from the experience and hopefully reach the other side relatively unscathed by it. At least when I had to make the final decision about having my second eye removed, the major decision about vision in the future was taken out of my hands. I could now put that constant nagging hope behind me. Sometimes we kick at doors that are not meant to be opened. I then tried, to the best of my ability, to work with what was left. I would never achieve great feats of athleticism or walk the length of Britain, or anything like that, but I would find achievement within my capabilities and boundaries.

While it's important to stretch ourselves, and overreach ourselves, we do have to keep focused on what is realistic. Set small goals for yourself, ones that are possible to reach and, as you achieve them, make your goals even greater. It is good to reach for the stars, but you can't stay in the clouds all the time. You have to face facts and face reality.

A prayer

Lord, many people this day will have to make momentous decisions. Many will face painful surgery that will be life-changing. Help them to face the challenges ahead. Help them to have the fight and the will to keep going. Give them the serenity of spirit, peace of mind and inner contentment, which is necessary to enable them not only to come to terms with what has happened, but to truly accept their fate.

13

A near-death experience

Six months on from the removal of my right eye, I was to receive another devastating blow. I went to see an orthopaedic surgeon due to the pain in my leg. He examined me and found that I had an abnormal pulse in both my legs, and he wished me to be seen by more specialists. The outcome was that I needed a bi-lateral lumbar sympathectomy. This surgical procedure would improve the circulation in my legs, by cutting the sympathetic nerve chain and getting rid of dead tissue.

This procedure is so much easier nowadays, but thirty-two years ago it was a very different ball game. I was exceedingly ill and had what I believed to be a near-death experience, although doctors didn't actually confirm that I had died. I had the sense of being lifted up from my hospital bed, heading towards the wall (by the way, in this situation I could see what was happening), going through the wall, down a long corridor which was tunnel-like, heading towards a light at the end, which was getting ever-brighter as I went forward. I heard several female voices, saying, 'You are coming to us.' Then a voice that was very definitely male said, 'Yes, you are coming but not yet, I have special work for you to do.'

I had no doubt that it was God speaking to me, and no doubt that he was male. Then I had the sensation of being drawn back down the long tunnel, and I found myself back in my hospital ward, which was a side room, looking down on the people in there – my mother and father, and various hospital staff. I could see and hear my mother crying, saying, 'She's dying.' I was aware of being sucked back into my body, which I could see lying on the hospital bed, and I wasn't happy. I enjoyed this wonderful freedom as I escaped from all my bodily restriction. I awoke screaming with the most incredible pain I've ever experienced. I pray that I'll never have to go through anything quite like it again.

For eight days I was on the critical list, receiving four pints of blood and four pints of plasma, being on morphine and other very strong painkilling drugs. But it appeared that the surgery had been a complete success. When I was *compos mentis* again, I realized I had been given a second chance. For now, I had no idea what special work God had for me to do, but I knew that I had to dedicate my life to the service of others. It may seem to you that I am speaking in elevated terms, thinking of my own importance – not so. This was a really genuine sense of knowing that my life was at a crossroads. I could either waste it or make something beautiful out of it. Time would tell and time did tell. In the most unexpected and wonderful way.

The one thing that this experience taught me was that I now never needed to fear dying. It was a most wonderful dream-like state that had the most amazing sense of freedom about it. Freed from worldly restriction, freed from the limitations within my body, I felt at that moment that I could just sprout wings and fly in the most incredible way. This was not drug induced. It was a real sense of my body and my spirit letting go, and I loved it. My fear is not dying, but how death will come. I'm sure we all hope that it will come quickly and cleanly. If we're honest we all pray that we will die in our sleep. For many, sadly, that will not happen, but we just have to pray for courage and deal with whatever comes.

A thought

Life can change within the blinking of an eye. Take someone who suddenly experiences a severe stroke. One minute they are fit and well, with their life ahead of them. Then in the next moment their life is altered for ever. I'm reminded of the story of the rich fool in the Bible, when a wealthy man decides that he will build bigger and better barns in which he can store all his wealth and all his possessions. One night, God said to him, 'You fool! For tomorrow you will die.' It all depends what value you put on life and whether materialism, creating more and more wealth, and having many possessions is more important to you than the things that are much more solid, like the stability of genuine friends and being surrounded by people you love. These things will remain, whether we have wealth or not. Those people who depart when our wealth or our health diminishes were not worth knowing in the first place.

A prayer

Dear Lord, there will be many this day who will have to come to terms with life-threatening or life-changing experiences. Many who will face difficult surgery, where they experience great pain and suffering. When we go through something like this, help us to get through our dark valley and come out on the other side. If we're fortunate to be given a second chance, help us to capitalize on it. Help us not to waste the time that we have been given, but to create something beautiful for you. Help us to use this time to really value the small things. The infinitesimal detail of nature. The joy of friendship. The importance of a comforting hand, both given and received. Help us to use what skills we have wisely, generously, and to come out of this dark experience renewed and refreshed, despite what we have just been through.

14

New beginnings

While I was having the operation on my back, the man who was my fiancé at the time came into the hospital and broke off our engagement. We attended the same church and, due to the emotion of it all, I felt I would not be able to attend services there if he was still a member of the congregation. So I spoke to a friend who was a Methodist minister, and he invited me to worship at his church, which I duly did. I had qualified in psychotherapeutic counselling, but as yet did not have a client caseload of my own. So all my hopes and dreams about a pending marriage and new job had gone down the tubes.

My life was in tatters. I took courage in both hands and started to attend worship on a regular basis at the Methodist church – and loved it. Almost three years on, I was sitting in the pew after the evening service, which had been extremely pleasant but not exactly compelling. I sat there quietly waiting for a friend to help me out of the church to go home. I suddenly felt a hand on my left shoulder.

'Hello. Who is there?' I said turning around.

A voice that was very deep and echoing replied, 'You have got to get off that pew, go to the front of the church and witness for me.'

I had no doubt at all that it was God speaking.

'Who me, Lord?' I exclaimed. 'You must be joking! Why would you want me with all the problems that it would cause, when there are so many able-bodied people who could do the job far better?'

I knew I couldn't ignore this. If I did I would do so at my peril. I had a feeling of elation and incredulity, all at the same time. Why me? then became Why not me? Recognizing that there would be many logistical problems, a preacher who was blind and in a wheelchair, would be quite difficult for church officials to get their heads around. But I always said that I was here not to comfort the afflicted, but to afflict the comfortable!

It would be great to make worship fully inclusive. All too often there is an attitude of seeing people with disability, or long-term illness, as objects to be prayed over. That is completely wrong because we are not sick or objects of pity. We have a right to be there as much as anyone else. If we believe that every person matters to God, then we could say that people with special needs need a little extra special care. The fact that I would be preaching from a wheelchair using Braille and, if you like, being an audio-visual aid for God, would be quite a powerful message to those who believe that God is a sort of 'Jim'll Fix It'. That he can make it 'all come right'. Perhaps in God's rich pattern it is not meant to come right. Maybe I would be able to do far more with my limitations than some able-bodied people, who spend their life rushing around and never quite getting there. For the moment I decided to keep all these thoughts in my heart. I had to internalize them, come to terms with them, and work out for myself just how committed I was to the call.

Three weeks later, when the feeling had not gone away, I decided to speak to my minister. His response was, 'Think carefully as it would mean a great many years of dedication and study.' In his opinion, I was already doing God's work with my work for disabled people. So, therefore, I should take a month to consider my position before making the next move.

One month went by and I realized that my wish to preach was not a desire but a compulsion. I felt compelled to witness for God from my wheelchair. I had gone over the many scenarios and difficulties. They did not put me off; they made me all the more determined. At a meeting with my minister I explained this. His response was that he had better give me a note to preach, which is the first step to becoming a fully accredited local preacher in the Methodist Church.

A thought

We are always told that when God calls us, it is a life-changing moment. It is a remarkable one and, so often, we are called not in a dramatic manner, but in a quiet, calm way. That call is never without sacrifice but it is with a great deal of hope and blessing.

A prayer

Lord, when you call let our hearts and minds be open. Let us hear clearly what you have to say, and help us to act on it. We realize that whenever you call us it will be that crossroads moment. That call may come out of a time of suffering, pain or deep sorrow. Yet it will be one of the most enriching periods in our life. Help us to heed that call and not shy away from it. Help us to be strengthened, renewed and refreshed, and help us to reach out to others. Not so much by what we say, but by the way we choose to live our life, in Christian witness, living by your example of the teachings of Christ. Help us to have that sense of morality and integrity, living by Christian precepts, which is so lacking in our world today. And help us to be proud to be one of your children.

15

Dogged determination

I had a mixed reaction from people when I entered the local preachers' meeting. I was questioned by the secretary as to my ability to preach. He said that it would be difficult for me to cope with the public speaking. I explained that I had done over three hundred radio broadcasts and some television, and had spoken to large audiences on the subject of disability. Public speaking would not be a problem.

'You may have problems with study,' he replied.

I told him of my O levels and my qualification in counselling.

'Oh, you can learn then!' was his response.

If I had not been a committed Christian, I would have thumped him one at this point! How would I break down this level of prejudice? The only way was to keep going with a tenacious spirit. I suppose it was a way of testing my resolve to preach. While I didn't have any counselling clients at this point, I was still in supervision. All counsellors worth their salt have therapy and supervision. My supervisor was very sympathetic and understanding over the fact that I wasn't given a caseload of clients from the foundation where I trained.

One day, she asked me how I felt about the situation.

'I feel as though no one is listening and nobody cares,' I said, 'and I'm banging my head against a brick wall.'
'Ah yes, but won't it be wonderful if, while you're banging your head,' she replied, 'the bricks start to tumble off the top?'

All these years later, I think I have finally demolished the wall, broken down so many barriers, and now there is a sense of freedom and space that was not there before. It's so easy to build walls of prejudice and have preconceived ideas about people. The assumptions that we make about another human being are terrible, and unnecessary. The old saying 'Don't judge a book by its cover' is very apt in this case.

My parents were extremely disparaging over my aspirations.

'You and your big ideas,' they would say. 'They all come to nothing and will get you hung one day.'

I felt this was quite appropriate when one thinks of Christ on the cross. His aspirations to teach a new way of living were frowned upon by the vast majority of people, and he suffered as a consequence. So why should I care? Why should I not just go where the spirit took me, and wait to see what would happen?

My mother worked in the same city bank as I did, and she was coming up for retirement in 1983. She had been on hand to give me physical support to get around the building and cope at meal times, coffee breaks and comfort stops. Now, with her pending retirement, the bank officials were anxious. This was before the days of assistance to work paid for by Jobcentre Plus. Behind closed doors my mother had negotiated with the bank management that I would be retired on medical grounds at the same time as she left. One day I was brought into the manager's office and told this was going to happen, and that my mother had already signed the necessary papers. I was furious. I didn't want to retire at thirty-three years old. I wanted the opportunity to interact with my work colleagues, discover myself and be my own person, without my mother sitting at my elbow. Now, all that had gone and I would be forced to leave the bank, albeit with a pension and a golden handshake, when I'd had no previous intention of doing so. I was devastated.

It is incredibly frustrating when people take charge of your life due to disability, when you are quite capable of making your own decisions. My mother thought that the best option I had was a life-long pension (I have to say all these years on that it has been exceedingly helpful). But self-esteem, pride, self-actualization and credibility to me, are, far more important.

Those who care for us have a great deal of 'control' over us. It reaches the point where they almost become you. If your carer doesn't wish you to do something, and you can't do it for yourself, then it doesn't happen. All people with disability should be allowed to make whatever decisions they can, however small. It may be as basic as what they will wear and what they will eat, what time they get up in the morning, and what time they go to bed. However basic, they should have the freedom of choice. In this situation, I had no choice. It was a fait accompli. Signed, sealed and now delivered. I was forcibly made redundant, with little prospect, it would seem, of regaining employment. What on earth would I do now? All I could do was concentrate on my studies as a preacher – and pray.

A thought

Life contains the most unexpected barriers. If we allow them to become our fortress it will be one of the most destructive acts that we could ever do against ourselves. Many of us put up barriers with our emotional conflicts that have not yet been resolved. It's the most wonderful feeling when we realize that as we take the bricks off the wall, one by one, and allow people to reach us, we find freedom. So often, when we battle against bitter and abject disappointment, it does feel as though we are banging our heads against a wall. Sometimes, we have to allow ourselves to be still and stop the pain and frustration, and just let time take its course. Maybe even five minutes at a time.

A prayer

Lord, there will be many this day who will experience the devastation of sudden redundancy. Everything they held dear shattered in an instant. Lord, the shock of this is unimaginably

16

Treading water

————•◦•————

I used this limbo period in my life to study and stretch my mind. My family thought it was a complete waste of time, but when you read C. G. Jung, Freud, Ardler, T. A. Harris and many more, then on the religious front many books from the great writers and philosophers of their day, it is wonderful. For those of you who have easy access to the printed word, you probably don't fully appreciate how restricting and difficult it can be to only have a limited selection of key books. Nevertheless, these are all great treasures to be prized. So my life took on this rather studious turn.

I was by now what is known as a preacher on trial. That meant that I attended worship with a more experienced preacher, who then let me conduct certain parts of the service. This was quite a nerve-wracking experience. When one is in the vestry, preparing for the start of the service, having preacher's prayer time with the steward, then receiving their blessing as you go forward through the doors of the church to stand, or sit in my case, in front of your congregation, it's awesome.

During this time I made some extremely good friends, who used to collect me for morning or evening worship. By now I had moved with my family to Hornchurch in Essex, and had to get used to a whole new set of people. This was challenging. It was in one of the Essex circuits where comments were made, by the secretary of the preachers' meeting, about my ability to execute my obligations in the pulpit.

By now I had begun to pass my preacher's examinations: Old Testament, New Testament, Christian Doctrine and Worship and Preaching. All my pass marks were between B+ and C, equal to candidating for the Methodist ministry. It was in the days when the preaching study was far more arduous than it is now. I can remember completing ninety one-thousand word essays over the period of years that I trained to be a preacher. This was a time of great spiritual growth, dedication and commitment to the call. It certainly wasn't something to be taken lightly. Years later, I can recall supporting a young preacher. He felt that he was so inspired that he didn't need to prepare. When I asked him why he hadn't adequately completed his preparation on one particular biblical study, which was the theme for the preaching the following Sunday, his answer was that he was waiting for divine inspiration. I learnt to my cost that unless you work at something the divine inspiration doesn't come. The way I worked at it was to read the given text for the lectionary, over and over again, until key words jumped out at me or I was given the idea of the sermon. It only came by hard work and dedication, but the rewards were tremendous.

Through visiting the churches on the circuit, I came into contact with people from all walks of life and in need of support. This is where my counselling training, and the skills that I had acquired, came into play, and I was able to help so many people. Gradually, my counselling client base was growing, although I hadn't deliberately set out to develop a practice. But people were coming to me and they were benefiting. The concept of the 'wounded healer' comes into play here. People recognized the advantage of coming to someone who had struggled, been there themselves and bought the t-shirt. They knew when I said 'I know how you feel', that I really did. It's so important to have walked the walk. Again, I could see God's rich pattern doing its delicate interweaving in what was going on in my life at this time. It was a case of just being patient and waiting to see what would come.

A thought

No education on any given subject is ever wasted. Anything we learn stretches the brain, broadens our mind and helps us to be a more rounded and whole individual. It's wonderful when we are able to show genuine interest in people's careers. Not necessarily because we understand what they do, particularly if it's a very technical subject, but because we are fascinated by people. Life is all about outreach and interaction. Without that we will not be good social animals. We will lack social skills and, more importantly, confidence.

A prayer

Lord, when we feel that we are treading water, expending time, help us to use our idleness profitably. Help us to value education in all its forms. Help us to grasp it, soak it up like a sponge and enjoy it for its own sake. Help us to see when things are not happening at the pace we would wish them to, that you are in this, you are there, guiding and shaping our future. Help us to know that while we have to work at things, we can't open doors until they are ready to be opened. Help us to be still and know that you are with us at every turn.

17

A new career

My good friend, Dr Wendy Greengross, known to many of you as Dr Wendy in the *Sun* newspaper and for her counselling broadcasts on the BBC's *If You Think You've Got Problems* programme, had become a great supporter to me from 1976, when I had my first eye removed. She had watched as I grew in confidence with my counselling training and my preaching studies. Wendy was devastated for me when I was retired from the bank at the age of thirty-three. She felt this to be a terrible waste, and I knew she would do everything she could to help.

One day, she told me of a new project that she was involved with: namely, setting up a database of all the residential care homes around Britain, charting their facilities, then matching these against potential residents. Everything was in place. The offices in Camden, London, were secured and the computer system was up and running. The only thing she did not have was a trained counsellor to interview the patients and their families, and talk to them about their preferences. It was one of those 'eureka' moments when she thought, 'Why didn't I think of this before?' and offered me the job as counsellor to Carematch, the residential care consortium. Of course I grabbed it eagerly. The only problem was that I would need someone to help me read the paperwork. I sought the help of the local volunteer bureau, and a retired business woman was found to help me fill out the necessary forms. Betty became a tremendous friend and took me out and about in her car, which gave me back the socializing that I had greatly missed.

I did this work for five years. It was very rewarding because I was getting alongside people, sharing in their difficulties. There were occasions when, due to the fact that it took so long for a vacancy in a home to become available, the applicant passed away. Then when I was doing my follow-up calls three or six months later, I was talking to people who were distressed because they had been bereaved. It was not uncommon for me to deal with something in the region of nine calls in an afternoon, with people in this situation. It was tough, but my counselling skills and my love of God really came to the fore. Of course, frequently I was asked why God allows such suffering. It's not that God causes or allows suffering, it's that God is with us, sharing in that pain, enabling us to get through.

There's no easy answer, and glib words do not help. Sometimes it's right and fitting that we own our anger. As a counsellor it's vitally important that I personally give permission for clients to express their anger. Frequently, the 'real' response should be 'If I were in your position, I'd feel angry too'. Then the client realizes that it's safe to express anger, and thereby grow. If I had not had my counselling training all those years ago, I would never have been able to do this work. But I found it a privilege to share in so many people's lives and get alongside them at a most difficult time.

A thought

We spend our life rushing around, trying to make everything come right. We have to own that there will be circumstances in which, however much we busy ourselves, we can't change the situation. When we meet someone who is bereaved, or a person who is terminally ill, we try so often to make platitudinal statements and busy ourselves around them, when sometimes all they want is to be held. Or to have you sit down beside them and be still. We can never really know the power of silence, the gift when somebody says, 'I'll leave you but when you need me

I'm here.' Or the silent hug that says it all, yet not a single word has been spoken between you.

A prayer

Lord, when circumstances are difficult, when the people we know and the people we love are distraught, help us to be there, holding, nurturing, loving. Help us to be their rock when everything around them seems to have shattered. Help us to speak when it's appropriate, and be quiet when it's not. Help us not to worry about filling their void, but stay with it. Help us to feel the power of silence and know that you are in that silence, loving them through it.

18

Shared dark valley

Every new contact with counselling took me on a different pathway. Through the work with Carematch, Dr Greengross asked me to get involved with SPOD (Sexual Problems of Disabled). It is sobering for some people to realize that people with disabilities are sexual beings too. Because they sit in a wheelchair it doesn't mean that they are sexually dead from the neck down. They have the same feelings as the able-bodied. This might be an area where I could specialize. I started to study this issue and attended various conferences. Again, this didn't go down too well in my household, especially when I was reading fairly explicit literature. However, the recognition of a person's sexuality is so important to their general well-being.

There are very few counsellors working out there in the field who deal with this issue. So I was beginning to get a number of referrals. My caseload was growing. Then I was approached to run a bereavement counselling course for volunteers. I didn't know that through this contract my life would be dramatically changed a few years later.

It was wonderful working with a dedicated team, many of whom came from connections at Whipps Cross Hospital in London. Now I had Carematch, the church, the bereavement support group and SPOD. My goodness, I was branching out! I was now beginning to see what God's purpose was in all this. It was just a case of hanging on in there, working hard and supporting those who came into my midst. Then I was asked if I would be a counsellor for the leading disability newspaper *Spastics News*, later known as *Disability Now*, produced by what is now known as SCOPE. The Spastics Society, as it then was, had an incident where a person with cerebral palsy had committed suicide because he had no one to talk to about problems regarding his disability and sexuality. The man had left a letter stating how he felt. This was quite a revelation for such an organization – that there they were offering all manner of support, but mostly on a physical model, never really taking into account emotional needs. So, I started what turned out to be a twenty-three-year commitment.

From my home, I took calls ranging from simple problems, such as where somebody could buy a pair of trousers when they had one limb longer than the other, to talking about advancing disability to a prisoner who had a life sentence for murder, with the prison governor listening in on our telephone conversation. For that I had to be vetted before I could deal with the call. I found it a fascinating experience. Essentially, one can only be a counsellor if fundamentally you love people. My work also took me into the realms of marriage guidance counselling, so I was privy to all types of behaviour. When things were really bad, one felt you could almost sell tickets! But it certainly made me see life in all its forms and rawness.

A thought

We owe a great debt to the many people up and down the land who have solidly trained to enable them to support people in a more effective way. The work of a counsellor is exceedingly difficult, because they must always be non-judgemental, yet constantly reflecting, mirroring, trying to show the person, in an impartial way, how the client's behaviour is perceived.

Often, the reflection of that behaviour is not received too well by the client. It creates tension and anger, which has to be resolved and dealt with. There is some fantastic work going on, supporting many different groups of people. Without it there would be much more emotional deprivation and more mental health problems.

It takes courage to share your life with a stranger, although it is often far better than sharing it with friends or family. The advantage of this is that the person can leave the issues with someone else and walk away from them, gaining space to think and breathe, before returning to the issues and working them through.

A prayer

Lord, for all those people who are hurting, needing to seek the help of a counsellor, I ask your help and blessing.

Lord, for that person struggling, the hour with the counsellor is like a precious oasis of time, where they can be quiet and still. The counsellor also needs our prayers because they are working hard with the facts that are presented to them. They are trying to be non-judgemental in a judgemental world, and maintain objectiveness when the issues that are presented may not make them feel like that. So we pray, Lord, for both in this special relationship. That through their encounter they may have a greater enrichment of life, as each of them sees it.

19

A fine romance

My life was to take a dramatic turn in a way I could never have expected. I had had a client referred to me for bereavement counselling. We had shared nineteen hours. In that time he had gone through many emotions, talking about his late wife, who had died six months earlier from cancer, and his children and grandchildren, and his job at a London sugar refinery. All he cared about was his family and job.

I could tell we were making progress when I smelt the aftershave and heard the creak of new shoes. Bit by bit he realized there was a purpose in living again. To begin with I was trying to give him a structure to his day, and a reason for living. When I first met him he was at the point where he was eating food from the saucepan that he had cooked it in, because he couldn't be bothered. One of my first tasks was to get him to break that pattern, and then I set him other minor tasks, week on week. One day we shared a great deal of laughter because I had forgotten to switch on the lights, and he didn't like to tell me. When the rain came, and the thunder struck, and I jumped suddenly at the noise, he thought this was hilarious. He was beginning to understand what blindness really meant.

When I did my training as a counsellor, it was thought that my blindness would put me at a total disadvantage and be off-putting to the client. Much emphasis is made in the counselling relationship of maintaining eye contact between you and your client. Obviously, I wouldn't be able to do this. In reality blindness has not proved to be a disadvantage, but a great enhancement. It's my personal belief that when a person is struggling to hold back the tears, the last thing they want is someone maintaining eye contact with them. They want to be able to express those tears, in whatever way they feel comfortable. One day, as we covered old familiar ground that we had dealt with many times, I asked my client what his needs were. His response was that he didn't have needs. He lived his life through others. I later found this to be an extremely true statement.

As I have stated previously, my charitable work always ran alongside my professional work, so I occasionally had to change counselling appointments to enable me to do both. Ralph was no exception, but he had an enquiring mind, and asked how I managed to do this. Not without difficulty, as I obviously did not drive due to my blindness, was my response. Being the kind person that he was, he made an offer that if ever I was stuck for transport he would be willing to assist me. At the end of his nineteen weeks, he was sufficiently improved to take up the challenges of life again, and hopefully succeed. Sometime later, I was asked to teach a blind person how to read Braille, in a care home which was some fifteen miles from where I lived. The fares would be prohibitive, so I thought of Ralph, who readily came to my assistance, transporting me for four and a half months on a weekly or twice-weekly basis to the home.

Our friendship was developing, but I had no thought at that time of it being anything other than friendship. We started to socialize after leaving the care home, and it was great to get out. I had to check out whether he felt he would ever need me in a professional capacity. If this were so, I couldn't associate with him in any form. But he assured me that he was functioning well. So our friendship continued.

I think where our friendship scored was that for such a long time there was no emotional entanglement between us. It was purely getting to know one another, without any sexual interaction, building up a firm foundation that would be lasting to us both.

A thought

In this modern world of ours where it is commonplace for people to meet and have a sexual relationship from the first day, my view of the beginning of a relationship like this would probably seem boring and old-fashioned. If you believe, as I do, that the sexual act between two people should be a natural exploration of loving feelings that you both share, then the sexual act would be an act of reverence. It should be seen as truly loving, precious and meaningful, rather than the one-night stand that is just another conquest that means very little.

Truly loving someone is being wholly comfortable in their presence, not having to fill the space, but delighting in the simple pleasures that you share. Discovering all the nuances of the person that you're close to should be something that you relish. If there is a coming together of minds as well as bodies, and this is freely shared, then in my opinion it will be a lasting foundation between them.

A prayer

Lord, when we have a new encounter with someone that we feel might develop, help us to start this relationship from the premise of respect and care. Help us to be on our best behaviour, for want of a better word, so that we start this relationship in gentleness, kindness and loving concern. Through these ideals help us to grow and blossom. Help us to enjoy every new and precious moment that we share. May the coming of love between us be so powerful and strong that nothing can separate us.

20

A coming together

Our friendship blossomed. We had many happy social hours together. It was wonderful helping Ralph to enter into the world of classical music. It was at one such concert, which had the romantic double bill of Tchaikovsky's *Romeo and Juliet*, and Rachmaninov's Second Piano Concerto, that I realized I was falling in love with this man, even though up to now there had never been any real intimacy between us. During the Rachmaninov piece I felt so tense inside and overwhelmed with feeling that I could hardly breathe.

On the way home in the car, I tentatively put my hand towards his, and he responded by gripping my fingers tightly. It was difficult for me because I didn't know if my feelings were completely unfounded. After all, I might have been picking up the wrong signals, and hoping for something that wasn't there. What if I had completely misread the situation? As a blind person I didn't have the visual signals. I just had to take things slowly and hope that I hadn't put my foot in it.

There was only one way I could find out and that was to test the water. Thankfully I'd guessed correctly. Later on during the journey home, Ralph pulled the car into the verge and drew me to him. The time we shared was extremely passionate and an expression of many hours of unexpressed pent-up feeling between us. We were both extremely tearful, and it was clearly obvious in that moment just how much we meant to each other. That tender time we shared together was extremely precious.

For the first time I realized that he had a moustache. I hated moustaches! But for now I would just have to get over my feelings. From that time on, our friendship grew and became truly special. We were as one, longing to be with each other.

I can remember one occasion when Ralph suddenly told me that he loved me. And I asked him not to use that word lightly, or glibly, but to make sure that he truly did before he said it. Of course there were many issues that we had to overcome. Not least of all how his children would respond to me, and how Ralph would cope with a wife who had disability. This was for the future. For now, we just delighted in each other's companionship, wanting to be with each other whenever we could. I loved the social life that I was beginning to experience, and I was blossoming as a woman who had found true happiness and wholeness.

For the first time in my life I had found someone who truly accepted me, with all my limitations, and had learnt to love me for them and love me through them. It was fabulous.

A thought

We're caught up by how we're perceived by others, what image we present to the world, and somehow we feel the enormous pressure of having to be perfect, of conforming to social norms and social expectations. For the most part, people who are unable to chase around and meet conventional obligations are either frowned upon at best, or completely rejected at worse.

It's great when we're able to present ourselves as a unique individual, and stand out from the crowd. Does it really matter if we don't conform? Can we not be unique, maybe even sometimes a little eccentric? After all, the world needs colourful people.

A prayer

Lord, for all those who are starting out on a new relationship, bless them and hold them to yourself. Help them to realize that this moment in their life is uniquely special and precious. It's said, Lord, that love is blind. It's wonderful when imperfections can be accepted for what they are. A beautiful body doesn't necessarily make a beautiful person.

Lord, often the people who feel inadequate, unloved and unwanted are the ones who have most to give. Help people to find the true qualities in each other. The qualities that really matter for a long, happy and lasting life together. Be with them as they truly discover each other, and help them to grow in love and friendship.

21

A time of discovery

A romance, in the truest sense of the word, is a wonderful time of discovery – a meeting of minds and bodies, of personal strengths and weaknesses, and of tenderness between a couple. In my case, Ralph had many moments of discovery about issues relating to disability. Yet he coped with them all, took to them like a duck to water, and delighted in them. We gave ourselves plenty of time to work out the strength of our own feelings towards one another, before we shared with others the fact that our friendship had become much more.

Many people had their own opinions, not all of them helpful, but we went on. Ralph would say that he was not sure where this relationship was going. He was worried that if he broke it off that it would hurt me deeply. I let him know, in no uncertain terms, that it might be me that ended the relationship, and he should not think of himself as my 'knight in shining armour', but respect me as an equal human being. He said that the thought that I might leave him took the wind out of his sails! And that only served to make him realize that he loved me more.

Our love grew stronger and deeper, and had a rock-solid foundation, which I felt was unshakeable. Before we could contemplate marriage, I felt it was important that Ralph care for me for forty-eight hours, by himself, so that he could never say that I hadn't prepared him for caring for a disabled person. We went to the home of a great friend of mine, who left us to cope. The following day Ralph asked me to marry him. My response was that I would be honoured.

That may seem old-fashioned, but it should be an honouring of the person you love and want to share your life with. This is a completely special time, and should be treated as such. Having crossed that barrier, there were more interesting things to discover. I realized that I loved nothing more than planning for our future, talking things through. I received far greater pleasure from the planning than from the achieving, as I loved to do 'blue-sky thinking' and see it all come right.

Although Ralph had his own property, I thought it was important that we started our married life together in a completely new and neutral place. We had great fun going around looking at houses and eventually choosing our first home together. When Ralph moved in six weeks before our wedding, so that he could complete the patio and ramped area at the back of the house, I delighted in being among the chaos, and the packing cases. My family were there too, wanting to take me away from it all, in case I should fall over something. But I wanted to stay for as long as possible, because this was a very important moment in both our lives.

When Ralph gave me the keys to the front door, I was overjoyed. I didn't care tuppence about the chaos. It was wonderful. Sending family 'packing' and having a cuddle surrounded by packing cases was very special. I didn't want the joy to end. I was discovering what being married to this man would be like, and I loved it.

A thought

Perhaps the two key words to any relationship are respecting and honouring. Respecting an individual in all aspects of their life is very important, as of course is mutual respect. The honouring should be the honouring of each other on a physical level, as well as on an emotional and mental level. So that you become one. Experience the joy of discovering all manner of things about this individual, and delight in it. It's not your job to change someone. None of us has the right to change an individual.

They have to change because they want to come nearer to you, and think in a more united and shared way.

I believe it's vitally important when someone has been married before, particularly if they have been bereaved, that the new couple start their lives together on neutral ground, so that the home is thought of as theirs, not the previous partner's. The 'new' person in this relationship needs to feel wholly comfortable with the situation, delighting in the discoveries that he or she makes about their partner.

The planning of your future life together should be a joyous discovering. Don't see this as the drudgery bit that has to be endured. This is the fun. Enjoy it for what it is.

A prayer

Lord, as the couple start their life together, strengthen them in the ways of mutual respect and admiration for one another. Let it be a time of great blessing. Let other people's opinion not spoil what they are discovering between them. For, Lord, it has nothing to do with anyone else how the couple choose to live their life. Let this couple's life be an example to those they meet. Let others delight in sharing in their life and enjoy their company, and make them truly happy. At one with each other, and at one with you.

22

Wedding day

The frenetic preparation on the morning of my wedding day hardly gave me any time to think about what I was undertaking. The whole day put me in a whirl. I can remember my mother asking me at six o'clock in the morning whether I had any regrets. I told her I couldn't wait. It wasn't that I wanted to be unkind, I was just being true to myself. I couldn't believe that it was really happening, until the Rolls Royce pulled up outside the house to take me to the church. What if Ralph had cold feet and didn't show?

I should have known that that was a ridiculous thought to have. Knowing Ralph he would be there far too early. I decided I had better go into the church in my wheelchair. But after the ceremony I hoped that I would be able to walk out, using my sticks, on Ralph's arm. For those who have never really studied the words of the marriage service, they are, if you choose to look at them, incredibly powerful. They really are a charter of commitment to that person that you are marrying. Those words 'For better, for worse, for richer, for poorer, in sickness and in health, till death do us part' are perhaps one of the biggest statements of commitment that we'll ever make.

When our minister said the words 'In sickness and in health' I was tempted to say 'Pass'. But I resisted. I spoke clearly and deliberately, because I wanted everyone present to know that I was making my vows with due thought and deliberation, and public commitment before God, and before the congregation.

Ralph was an incredibly shy person, and I know he spent many days of anguish over the words. In the end, it all went without a hitch, and it was a day in my life that I will always remember and cherish. It was the start of a new life, a new love – a love that is totally different from parental love, which is equally important and has its place in the scheme of things. Yet, from our own personal evolution, the love you have for your partner is completely and fundamentally different.

The wedding day is a rite of passage. A new beginning. It was a remarkable day, a day that I thought would never happen, because I never thought that anyone would be mad enough to take me on. I never thought that anyone could love my body with all its imperfections. But Ralph cared nothing about those. He just loved me unconditionally and for me. Our honeymoon took place in the city of York, and we spent a wonderful week wandering around the Yorkshire Dales and visiting the various places of interest. There was nothing more marvellous than sitting in the Yorkshire Dales, having a champagne picnic, which had been provided by the hotel. I drank in every moment of it, because every moment was so special.

I know I use that word 'special' often. But I could never truly explain to you just what a time it all was. I would have to come down to earth with a bang very soon, and get back to normal life. But for now I delighted in the company of this man, who wanted nothing more than to be with me. I was determined that when we got back, our home would be a place of welcome, which we would freely share with others.

It would be a place of love, kindness and gentleness, and where people would find a welcome whenever they came, or with whatever problem they chose to share with us. I never wanted people to feel that we didn't have time for them. Ralph was great at stretching the meal to another one or two people. I would get him on one side and ask him if we had enough to make two more meals. He would laugh and say 'You and your stretching!' but it worked. There was so much love and openness in this home, and people wanted to be with us. And that was magic.

A thought

Love and success are not dependent upon materialism. It doesn't matter where you are, or what social status you have. The most important aspect is that you are together, freely sharing with one another, that you have a togetherness that is clearly visible to all of those around you. Love doesn't have limits. There is always enough love to go around, and enough love to be freely shared. A home without love is not a home. It's just a building, a place to lay one's head and keep the rain out.

A prayer

Lord, let the love that the couple share blossom and grow. Help them to not be caught up by materialism, but value the things that really matter. Let their home always be a place of welcome, where their love may be freely shared. Let their arguments be settled before sleep, in love and mutual respect for one another.

23

A new life together

The wedding and honeymoon were fantastic. But I now had to face the harsh reality of learning to cope on my own during the day, for the first time in thirty-seven years. Occasionally, people would pop in, but for the most part I was by myself, and I was terrified. Ralph, bless him, agonized as he left our home in the morning, and checked that I was all right immediately he arrived at work. He never criticized me when I made a mess of things – sometimes there were more objects on the floor than on the table. And for many of my mishaps we just laughed about them. I worked hard to give him a happy homecoming. The coffee on, the fire lit and his favourite music on the hi-fi, with the evening meal prepared and in the oven.

My biggest problem was remembering to put the lights on and pull the curtains on winter evenings, as I used to forget and the nights drew in early. Ralph said that when you have spent so long by yourself, then suddenly you put your key in the door, call out and you receive a happy, welcoming response, it's marvellous. I breathed a sigh of relief once he came through the door. I just wanted him with me. I needed to feel safe, and I wanted to make a real home for us both.

We struggled in this way for two and a half years. All the while our life was evolving with my preaching commitments coming to a climax for my accreditation, just one year after we were married. Then Carematch lost its funding by the Greater London Council and I was made redundant. What would I do now? What direction would I take? Fortunately, I had Ralph supporting me in all my endeavours and he was wonderful. He had a saying that for me is so meaningful: 'There's no shame in trying and failing – the shame is not trying at all.' I knew he would back me whatever I did, even if I fell flat on my face. He was my rock, my strength. For the first time in my life I had someone I could lean on. My biggest problem was that Ralph wanted me to lean on him to the point of making him fall over, and I was a strong woman mentally, if not physically. I had to be, because I had to face so many difficult challenges and learn from them, and grow.

I'm sure there were many who did not give our marriage a chance. They thought that we would fall at the first hurdle, or at the first major crisis. But when Ralph was involved, crisis brought out the best in him, and you found that you'd coped with it and come out on the other side. He was fantastic at appreciating the little things that showed him how much I cared. I always joked and said that I wouldn't really care if I lived in the garden shed, as long as we were together. And that is truly how I felt.

A thought

There will be many people getting married and setting up home together. Tremendously challenging but terrifying nevertheless. It's difficult when one has to be responsible for another person, considering their needs rather than one's own. The old saying that you never know someone until you live with them is so true. It will always be the little things that really annoy. Like the squeezing of the toothpaste in the middle of the tube. But it's necessary to keep in focus the real reasons why you set up a life with this person. What the lasting qualities would be and why you love them in the first place.

A prayer

This meditation depicts two aspects of a life. A life that was lonely then found fulfilment. For the couple starting out afresh, give them a sense of joy and wonderment of it all, as they plan a life together and the possibility of children. Help them to appreciate the little things in life that actually make a marriage special. Be with them in times of crisis, strengthening, guiding and supporting, and help them to know that this relationship has three of you in it.

24

Go forth and tell

----◆◆◆----

Seven years of study and preaching commitment were now to culminate in a service commissioning me as a fully accredited Methodist local preacher. What a moment. A day I had longed for. I can remember the beautiful summer's evening the day before, warm yet cool. Ralph had invited me to be with him in the garden while he cut the lawn and did one or two jobs outside. Fatal mistake one! I had forgotten those awful little mozzies, who shout 'whoopee' when they see me and think it's a rather large meal that they can enjoy.

In the space of fifteen minutes I had been bitten fifteen times on each leg. The following day Ralph put my compression therapy stockings on for me before he went to work, and I was suddenly aware that my leg was getting hotter and hotter. On Ralph's return from work, he looked at my leg and called the doctor at once. Eventually he arrived, giving me large doses of antihistamine which made me like a zombie. I was really upset, as I thought I wouldn't be able to make the service. Ralph said that he would carry me on a stretcher if it was necessary, but he was determined I would get there!

The church was full. Many people had come from different parts of the country to wish me well at this special moment in my life. Typically, the Methodist hymn singing was great, raising the roof. Hymns that were especially important to me were 'Go forth and tell! O church of God, awake!' and 'Take my life, and let it be consecrated, Lord, to Thee'. This was an incredible moment of commitment, and dedication, to the service of God through the spoken and written word of a preacher. It wasn't for me to think that I was important, rather that I was a channel, a vehicle by which I could communicate God's word and his love. It was a very special period in my life. The responsibility of a preacher is awesome, because we never know how the words we say will affect another human being. Certain words or subjects may seem quite innocuous to one individual, yet to another are very painful. So, one always has to be mindful of why we are there and how we affect others.

The pastoral role, for a preacher, is also vital in terms of ministry. Now I wasn't just the wife of Ralph, but I was one of the local preachers within our Methodist circuit. As such I was the property of the local community. Ralph said he sometimes found it difficult to share his wife with so many, but secretly I think he was proud. The presiding preacher that day was the Revd Brian Goss. He referred to me as an audio-visual aid for God. What a privilege.

A thought

In this secular world of ours it's difficult to stand up and be counted for a Christian belief. Christian commitment, and all the responsibility of that, can often set us apart from others, because we do not always want to be part of the crowd. It's vitally important that we stand up for what we believe in, and are proud to call ourselves a member of the family of Christ. Part of that commitment is to reach out to others in care and neighbourliness, pick up on people's isolation, give them time when they are bereaved and lonely. Often to the detriment of our own needs. For the commitment of being a follower of Christ is also about committing your life to others.

A prayer

Lord, for all those people who are seeking a new way, discovering the Christian faith and what it means to be committed to it, bless them. Lord, for those who are expressing the word in terms of the commitment of preaching, hospital chaplaincy, chaplaincy within the services, give them strength to speak your words adequately in difficult circumstances. To all those trainee preachers working towards their accreditation, combining study and full-time work, give them a sense of determination to complete the task, and a true sense of privilege in transmitting the word.

25

Building blocks for God

———•◆•———

We were at the stage where Ralph was beginning to help me with some of my consultancy work. I was asked to appear on television. We had to go to Bristol for the recording. We stayed in a five-star hotel that was supposed to be wheelchair friendly, and have adequate facilities in the bathroom. Sadly, this wasn't the case. We came back from that trip absolutely shattered. While resting, my mind was working overtime, thinking of what we had just experienced and the lack of facilities that were available for people with disability. I suddenly announced to Ralph that when I died I wanted any money I have left to be put into a trust fund, to adapt hotel bedrooms for people with disability. Ralph thought this was a good idea, so we visited an old friend of mine, who was my legal adviser. He listened to what I had to say. Obviously, he would be able to organize this.

'Why on earth don't you set a trust up in your lifetime,' he questioned, 'where you could use your expertise of a double disability and make a difference to good effect?'

Ralph and I went home and talked through the idea. We assembled a team of eight people one night, each with their own particular skills, and we put a total of £1,150 together to enable us to seek the necessary advice to become a registered charity. Through discussion, we realized that it would be far better to raise money to purpose build a house for holidays, rather than adapt an existing building. That way we would not have to pay for mortgages. The Lin Berwick Trust was born on 18 August 1989, and it has been growing steadily ever since.

In the early days we were unknown. When I went out speaking with Ralph about this work, people gave us money and put their trust, and faith, in us. It was wonderful. Money was incredibly hard to come by, but we received our first big break when a tiny piece was written about me in the Saturday *Telegraph* Meditation. Eight thousand pounds dropped through my letterbox! Some of it wrapped in newspaper. When we had many letters we asked the next door neighbour to come and oversee the post. We had to make sure that everything was truly above board, because people were trusting us to do this work. If Ralph and I needed a purpose for our marriage and a fulfilment of the promise that we had made on our wedding day, that we would dedicate our marriage in some way to God, then this was it. We had no idea where this journey would take us. We had to be open to a real sense of discovery. But I knew, whatever we did, we had the opportunity to make a difference.

When I talked to people about the work, they said that the need is vast; one holiday house is not going to make that much difference. When there is a national appeal on television for feeding the hungry, in some war-torn or ravaged part of the world, we look at what we can do and it appears miniscule and insignificant in the general scheme of things. We tend to ask ourselves, 'What is the point? Our small donation won't make any difference.' The answer is that if everyone unselfishly makes a donation they also make a difference. The same principle applies with the work of the Trust. One house may not make a huge difference to the number of families who are affected by disability in some way. Yet if you can only help forty or so families in the course of a year, then to their particular lives we make a difference, albeit only for a week or a fortnight at a time.

A thought

Often we feel that the contributions that we are able to make in life are so inconsequential that they are useless. We never can tell how the things that we do will make a difference to a situation, or to someone's life. You could say that when Christ embarked upon his preaching and healing one man with twelve disciples wouldn't make much difference, given the difficulties of communication in those days. Yet, some two thousand years on, people are still captivated by his teaching, and want to be disciples of the faith. The things that we do in life, and how we affect others, are like ripples on a pool. We have no idea when what we say or do is going to change something. Yet, it is wrong to stand by and do nothing at all.

A prayer

Lord, when we try to express your love to others in outreach, we have no idea where that will take us. Help us to build something that is lasting and meaningful, that will give others a firm foundation. Help us to have a sense of community, a real sense of positive outreach. Help us to realize that life is not all about taking things for yourself, but about giving time, energy and expertise to worthy causes to create change and to make a difference.

26

One small step along the way

———•◦•———

Ralph regularly attended our local Methodist church. He had come a long way spiritually because now his visits were not just when I was preaching. When taking Holy Communion our minister always brought the bread and the wine to our pew and offered it to Ralph, as well as to me. Ralph usually shook his head and the minister walked away. But he never stopped offering it.

One day, Ralph accepted it. At the end of the service, our minister said to me how wonderful it was that Ralph had accepted communion for the first time. I was incredulous, happy and yet tremendously sad at the same time, because I had prayed at each communion service that Ralph would reach out and accept the bread and the wine, thereby asking Christ to come into his life. I had hoped that when it happened it would be a special moment that we could share. In the end he had chosen to make this commitment solely by himself.

The next step was for Ralph to start the training to be received into the church. While all this was going on, Ralph was preparing to take early retirement from work, so that he could devote more time to me and help me with my consultancy. His life was at a crossroads in more ways than one. We had no idea where it would take us. We didn't even know whether we would end up with enough money to live on, even though we had carefully done the arithmetic and thought it would work out. The minister asked Ralph whether he would like to give a testimony. He was absolutely horrified at this idea, yet on the day that he was received into membership, quite spontaneously he asked if he could say something. Ralph told the congregation how I had never forced religion down his throat, but had encouraged him to come in, particularly when it was cold outside. Ralph's response was that he wanted to be a member of the Christian family and know Christ personally.

Knowing how shy Ralph was, the whole congregation was overcome. Our minister gave Ralph a huge hug of welcome. It was a very proud day for me too. Was this part of God's rich pattern? If so, he was taking Ralph in very unexpected directions. Five years earlier, if you had said to me that Ralph would become a Christian, I would have said that there was more chance of pigs flying. However, when God has a hand in the decisions we make, the most unexpected things happen.

A thought

It's one of those heart-stopping moments, when we realize how God has become so important to us. When we take that first tentative step towards a new direction, it takes courage to own that leap of faith publicly. Yet it is fantastic when we know for sure that God is alongside us.

A prayer

Lord, when you call us, let our hearts and minds be open. Help us to hear your voice in this secular world. Help us to take up the challenge and own that you are part of our lives, and be thankful.

27

Up, up and away

---•·•·•---

The next five years were incredibly rewarding and challenging. As I grew in confidence as a married woman, I grew in my desire to explore the world around me, and Ralph was the one to help me to do it. His attitude of 'You're not disabled, you're just someone who needs a bit of help' was marvellous. He would try to let me go for any challenge that I wanted to take up. I had been studying homeopathic medicine for a little over a year, working towards a diploma. Then we decided to take our first trip abroad to Paris. I absolutely loved it and had the bug to travel. My next challenge was visiting Israel, which was incredible, bringing the Bible to life – enhancing it in some cases and spoiling it in others. When I read my Bible the Garden of Gethsemane was no longer that beautiful, peaceful place. It was now a noisy city complete with police sirens, camel traders and raucous bystanders. But I wouldn't have missed it for the world.

Later, we made trips to Scotland, Dublin and, to celebrate the passing of my first diploma in homeopathic medicine, one on Concorde. My wonderfully daft husband took as serious my tongue-in-cheek comment about celebrating my examination passes by going on Concorde, turning up with the ticket. I was incredulous – what an experience! I only wish now that I had purchased some of the Concorde memorabilia. The whole day was magical. The more I travelled, the more I wanted to grasp hold of these fantastic experiences. Something was to happen later on in my life that would prevent my exploration of the world around me.

We were doing wonderful things with Ralph's early retirement, not wasting any God-given moment. While it was brilliant having one's head in the clouds, one also had to come down to earth occasionally. Ralph was working with me in my role as a disability consultant. Since being made redundant, I had developed this side of my work. I was engaged by an agency to set up lectures and courses to highlight the needs of people with disability, and create change within the social services or social work setting. Ralph was a tremendous help with this, driving me to appointments and sometimes helping me with the lectures. If he had any fear about what he would do with his retirement, he could forget it. We had as much work as we could handle, and the income was a fantastic help.

Having a greater income meant that we had a far better social life. I know that my parents thought we were crazy when we spent money on weekend breaks at some lovely hotels, visiting many parts of the English countryside. Now, I don't regret a single second of the time we spent exploring the world around us. Ralph had already been to many of the places that he introduced me to. He said that my blindness made the visits feel new to him, as he was imparting information and getting me in touch with his world in a very different way, and he loved the challenge. He enjoyed helping me understand and experience what the world was like outside of my usual environment. I would worry because I was more reliant on him, asking him to help me with many more tasks, because of my blindness. He never complained, in fact I think he enjoyed being needed. We may have had a reduced bank balance – but what wonderful memories.

A thought

I have spoken many times about taking up the challenge and relishing it, enjoying the life around you and appreciating its beauty. Gaining finance in the bank is all very well but it doesn't bring happiness. The old saying 'There are no pockets in a shroud' is very meaningful. We can't take it with us. Money was meant to go around and be exchanged. It was never meant to be held on to, in a kind of 'Silas Marner' mentality. In *Silas Marner*, a book by George Eliot, Silas is a country weaver, who stockpiled his payment of gold coins and brought them out every night to look at them. Then one day they were stolen and his world fell apart, until a small child with beautiful golden curls walked into his cottage. Silas, who was very short-sighted, thought that the golden curls were his coins lying on the floor. Instead it was this beautiful child curled up. Silas cared for the child and brought her into womanhood. He had more friends and more fun than ever his money could have afforded. Later, his money was recovered, but his life had moved on. I think of the Silas Marner mentality when I realize the importance of doing things now, because tomorrow might be too late.

A prayer

Lord, we can be obsessed by saving for a rainy day. We can spend our life worrying about the decreasing value of bank interest or shares or savings, missing the real point that money is only useful if you can do something with it. Often in our world today we are driven by payment for what we do. Very few people do something for no reward. Lord, when we give of our time and energy to you to help someone else, perhaps the only reward we'll have is our own personal satisfaction, or the smiling face of another person. It's perhaps the best reward that we'll ever know.

28

A devastating moment

One morning I awoke to hear Ralph making some very strange noises, squealing and screeching sounds, and a noise from his mouth as though he were blowing bubbles. He couldn't speak to me and he couldn't move. My first thought was that he may have had a stroke. I dialled 999 and eventually help arrived, and Ralph was taken to hospital. I followed sometime later, and when I reached him in A&E, he was able to speak to me. I have never felt so grateful than at that moment. Whatever came later, the fact that we could still communicate was something to be incredibly grateful for.

As time went on Ralph completely recovered, and by late afternoon was able to walk out of the hospital. Further tests would need to be done, but for now we could go home and try to relax. Relax? That was impossible. My mind was working overtime. What would I do if Ralph was very seriously ill? My life would radically alter. I know it's selfish of me to talk about my life altering, when it was Ralph I should have been wholly concerned about. But, being human, you can't put your own concerns completely to one side, because your mind is racing, going fast forward, looking at worst-case scenarios, and wondering how on earth you'll both cope. After all, Ralph was my carer. Now, we were in a situation where he might need care himself.

On reflection, Ralph had been unwell for a little over a year. Doctors put it down to stress, although Ralph was insistent that he wasn't stressed. A series of medical tests followed, and thankfully he was still able to drive for the moment – vital in our case, as we needed wheels to be able to achieve anything.

Hospital follow-up visits continued. We were no further forward. Ralph experienced periods of great depression and anxiety, shaking violently. His wonderful sense of humour had disappeared and he never whistled any more. He dragged his feet around like someone who didn't have the energy to pick them up. What was going on?

I suspected Ralph had Parkinson's disease. On a subsequent visit to the hospital, I demanded that we were seen by a consultant neurologist. Staff were reluctant, but I insisted, refusing to leave until we did so. The consultant neurologist duly appeared. After little more than five minutes he was able to tell Ralph that he did indeed have Parkinson's disease. An MRI scan later confirmed this. The consultant said that the condition would render Ralph with mobility problems, unable to walk, having to use a wheelchair, and with difficulty with speech and swallowing.

'Whatever you want to do,' the consultant said, 'do it now.'

That told me that time was limited. I felt the ceiling meet the floor. Everything was closing in. All I could do was cry out.

'Oh no, not you, not this!' I cried. 'How could you do this to us, Lord?'

We went home totally shattered, surrounded by packing cases, as we were about to move to Suffolk. The property we were moving to had a very large garden. I didn't know how we would manage if Ralph could no longer tend his garden, which he loved. I was terrified for Ralph and terrified for myself.

I had dedicated my life to Christian service, and Ralph and I had offered our marriage in this way. Everything was fine, now our life was in tatters. I had no idea whether I could pick up the pieces and begin again. Ralph was now helping me when I preached, passing me hymn books, telling me the order of service and often helping me with the visual aid material for the children's address. What would happen here? How long did we have?

Ralph was fatalistic. He switched off in that doctor's office and never switched back on. It was as though I was pushing a forty-stone man up a hill. It was shattering.

A thought

There will be many people today who receive earth-shattering news, either because of the loss of a loved one, or because of terminal illness. When death is sudden we lose the opportunity of telling our loved one what they mean to us. We are then left with so much regret, so much unspoken business. This is particularly painful if the last thing they remember are unkind words that were said. How do we deal with that kind of loss?

In the case of long-term illness there is the chance to say what you feel for one another, how much you care and how much you love each other, and to do all the things that you wanted to do before the end. It's at times like this that you realize that money and materialism count for nothing. Money can help to buy health, but it depends on the circumstance. All money can do is speed up the medical process, it can't win in the end.

A prayer

Lord, when someone receives news that makes them feel as though the ceiling and the floor are caving in, be there holding their hand. When someone is facing the news of terminal illness, give them courage. Be with their loved ones who have to stand by and watch. Give those people the courage to be a rock in times of stress. Help them both to value every day that they are given. Help them to make the most of your God-given moments, and be thankful for what they have had, rather than focusing on what is being taken away.

29

Where was God?

———•◆•———

I couldn't pray, I could only cry out in anguish. Why Lord? Why did you allow this to happen? I had, I felt, experienced my own personal Calvary a number of times in my life, and now I was having more problems heaped upon me. So many of us feel that we are not strong enough to carry this kind of burden. The yoke is too heavy. It doesn't help when people say 'God only gives us what we can bear', or when they come out with platitudinal statements. What we need are people alongside us, sharing in the difficulty, and not walking away when life gets tough. I felt truly let down by God, completely and utterly numb. No words of Scripture were comforting. I was so shocked and shattered by the experience, that Scripture did nothing for me. Where was my God? He had been my rock, my strength. But he wasn't there. There was no sense of his presence, it was a total void.

As for preaching, I couldn't. Unable to preach because I couldn't say, with any sense of conviction, that God was a God of love. The strange aspect of all this was that I could pray for others, but somehow felt as though I had done something so bad, although I didn't know what, that I was being punished – punished because I loved someone so much. Perhaps it was wrong to care for another human being so deeply and not be able to sense your life without them.

Was this the terrible price I had to pay? Would it have been better never to have had the wonderful experience of truly loving someone? To be in a situation where you have to stand by and watch, or in my case listen, to someone else's anguish, and know that you are powerless to change it, is a terrible situation to be in. I have felt inadequate and a burden on people all my life. Now my own inadequacies were truly in evidence because I wouldn't be able to care for the man I loved. When the situation became desperate for him, other people would take my place. I couldn't bear this because I knew that I should be there, loving and caring for him until the end. But my own physical circumstances, and lack of vision, wouldn't allow me to do so.

I felt like screaming inside. My artificial eyes, which looked so real, were completely useless. What I needed now were eyes to see with. Instead of that, in terms of my husband's care and what was happening to him, I would be floundering in the dark. Night-times were the worse, when I would go to bed and lie there shaking as I thought about the future. I couldn't see a future. In fact, I didn't even care whether I lived or died. And, if I'm honest, I probably still don't.

People would quote the poem 'Footprints' to me on many occasions. But I didn't feel carried. In fact, I felt totally abandoned. How would I cope with the loss of this wonderful man? He hadn't died but I knew that what we had in terms of our life together was being cruelly taken away. The thought of that was completely and utterly devastating.

I tried reading my Bible but my mind was in a whirl. I was so angry that I literally threw the book across the room, or slammed it onto the floor. That isn't the way I would treat the Word, which was pivotal to my very existence. In the past I had always received great comfort from St John's Gospel, but those familiar words meant absolutely nothing. They were unconnected and, instead of being comforted, I would scream.

I felt so let down. I had been a Christian all my life and spent many years in Christian service working for people with disability. When I married Ralph we dedicated our marriage to God, in love, service and support, for all those people who came into our lives. We had helped so many along life's road – friends whose marriages had broken down, and others who needed support due to bereavement, for example. Now everything that we had striven for was going to be lost. This sounds like a 'If you scratch my back, I'll scratch yours' kind of statement. I don't mean it in that way. It's more about a real sense of dedication and now everything that I had believed in, and striven for, had been cruelly snatched away.

Ralph was, and will always be, the most important person in my life. He gave me purpose and meaning, and a reason for living. Now it felt as though I had none. I was going through the motions of daily life, and it was one huge drudgery. When I looked at the various passages in the Bible that spoke of God's love, I felt like tearing them up one by one. It was only the fact that I had always believed the Bible was a sacred book, and therefore shouldn't be defaced, that stopped me from doing it.

I tried and tried to read those words, but my mind felt utterly confused. It was as though I was in a thick fog, and I couldn't see my way out of it. I had no idea whether feelings of commitment would return, or how long it would take. I was truly in a spiritual desert.

A thought

It's easy to be comfortable with God when life around us is fulfilling and we are happy. When the going gets tough it's said that the tough get going. Then we feel like rejecting this faith that has been comforting. The crucifixion was anything but 'comforting'. When I tried to put myself in the position of how Christ must have felt on the cross, I couldn't imagine what must have been going through his mind. The people who flocked to him for healing, and a new slant on Scripture, suddenly turned their backs on him and were mocking him, and being violent towards him. What must he have felt like? He must have felt completely and utterly betrayed. Let down by the people he trusted, especially one of his disciples, who told on him to the soldiers by giving him a kiss. How betraying is that?

Christ cried out, 'My God, my God – why have you forsaken me?' So, why shouldn't we do exactly the same? Why do we feel that it is wrong? In crying out in anguish we often discover ourselves.

A prayer

Dear Lord, when we feel betrayed and rejected by you, give us a clear message that you are there. Help us to learn from our cries of anguish, that in speaking out our thoughts we may discover a new path towards understanding. Lord, it's not all about everything coming 'right'. Sometimes, you make your most powerful statements in helping us to work through our feelings when it isn't right. When life presents us with cruel happenings, such as terrible illness, we often don't have an answer. Perhaps we're not meant to. Perhaps you want us to see what we can learn through tragedy, and how we can be enriched by it.

Lord, your rich pattern is often mightily strange. I don't know what you're trying to prove, or what you expect us to do. But I do ask that whatever crosses we have to bear, you make us capable of carrying them. Help us not to be on our knees as a result, but enable us to stand up, hold our head high and still speak for you.

30

A reason for living

———•◦•———

Ralph hated the term Parkinson's disease. He felt he was some-how contagious, and didn't want anyone to know that he had it. He behaved as though he were ashamed. When tragedy strikes, our first reaction is that we don't want to go on. Life has no meaning. For us, there was meaning; our first holiday home, Berwick Cottage, for The Lin Berwick Trust, was about to be opened. What an achievement.

We came from totally different ends of the spectrum. Ralph's was shame, mine was, so what? You have Parkinson's disease – so what? You might end up in a wheelchair – so what? You have as much right to be in this world as anyone else. I can remember the enormous sense of pleasure I had when Ralph sat me on the ground at East Harling in Norfolk, so that I could feel the foundations of the building and the first three layers of bricks. The builder found this fascinating to watch because I was lovingly stroking the bricks. This was something tangible about our relationship; something lasting that would go on long after Ralph and I had left this mortal coil. Now we were almost ready for the opening – fantastic. When the walls were completed, and the roof was on, I had gone around the building and prayed in every section that God's spirit and presence would be in this building, and there would be much happiness. The builder said he had never seen anything quite like it. He had never seen anyone stroke the bricks and pray against them as I did. But I wanted this building to have an atmosphere all of its own. I wanted it to be a special place.

On the day of the opening, we had at least one hundred people to share in the special moment when Sue MacGregor cut the blue ribbon and declared Berwick Cottage open. There were just a handful of people who knew about Ralph's Parkinson's. There was no point in telling the masses, he wouldn't have wished me to do so. Our great day, just one day after our wedding anniversary, was tinged with such sadness for us. We had reached the summit of all our fundraising and had something there for all to see. It was going to make the lives of people with disability so much easier, if only for a week or a fortnight.

Now the man who had worked so hard for others was disabled himself. What would the future hold for us both? We had no idea. As with so many times in my life, triumph has gone alongside great sadness. I have seen the work of God in the tragedy, and that has been wonderful. Smiling faces to the public, but tears of extreme sadness in private. For now, one would have to put on a brave face, be public property for a while, and smile sweetly for the cameras.

When in my opening speech I said that this would be the first of many, because we weren't stopping at one cottage, there was a clearly audible groan from the assembled group. They knew me well – I would never be satisfied while there was still a need out there. I wanted our organization to make a difference. I was the person up-front – Ralph for now was the physical brawn, the man in the background, who kept my feet on the ground, instead of putting my head in the clouds. Yet he was so proud of the vision I had to change expectations. People with disability have as much right to a five-star lifestyle as anyone else.

A thought

So often when tragedy strikes we put on a persona, a mask for when we meet people. We smile and pretend everything is fine, when in fact we are breaking up inside. Sometimes, the more we laugh, the more we're really crying. Yet it's easier to say we're fine and move on, rather than explain.

A prayer

Lord, life is about building. Building blocks of understanding, giving us something to lean on and be strong for. Lord, we spend our life in a form of pretence. On the one hand, saying we're fine, on the other crying in anguish. Lord, this is a very fragile state to be in. Help us to be strong, hold us up when we are not capable of doing it for ourselves. Lord, help us to find a purpose for living when our life has been shattered. Help us to find spiritual renewal in the rubble that we find ourselves amongst. You are our foundation, our solid walls and roof. You are the means by which, when we come into your house, you make the house our home. Give us the welcome that we so richly need, and richly deserve. For you treat each and every one of us as your precious child, whatever mess we have made with our lives. Let your everlasting arms welcome us in love and friendship.

31

Patience through the chaos

———•◦•———

Living with Parkinson's (I use that phrase deliberately due to the fact that Parkinson's took over our lives) is no joke, particularly when the person suffering from it is angry, but will not express his anger. The way it manifested itself was to come out in all kinds of disruption and stubborn behaviour. The mood swings were incredible. Quiet and peaceful one moment, then irrational rage the next. Rather like the tantrums of a small child, although he wasn't.

What Ralph could do to a tidy kitchen was unbelievable. He was like a human tornado. His idea of 'tidying' in order to get rid of paper was to create more and more piles, not shred any of it, and then in desperation and boredom gather it all up, creating one huge pile again. The only difference was that something like eight hours would have gone by. Ralph deeply resented that his life revolved around taking pills. His life was totally dependent on the taking of these tablets strictly to time. I tried everything, such as a container that had the days of the week on the section, so that he would know whether he had taken his tablets at a given time of the day, an electronic pill box that bleeped to tell you when to take the tablets, which you then reset for the next dose, blister packs from the chemist – none of it worked. I knew all his medication like the back of my hand, up to as many as twenty-eight pills a day, and I knew when the medication had to be taken. I would remind him, and he would go into the bedroom to get the pills. Several hours later, due to his behaviour, I would realize that he hadn't taken them. When I asked why, he would say, 'Because I choose not to.'

Then he would plant himself in front of the oven, fridge or hob and decide that he wasn't going to move. As for cooperating, in terms of helping me to cook the evening meal – forget it.

My day of frustration started at six o'clock in the morning and went on until past midnight every day. Each day I prayed it would be different, that we would have a better day tomorrow, but sadly that was not to be. I longed for sleep. We would go to bed, settle down, snuggle up towards one another, me cuddling him so that he would feel less anxious and hopefully drop off to sleep. I would be praying for us both that we would get some sleep. Just as I was about to drift off, Ralph would decide he either couldn't stay there, and would get up, crash his way through the doors into the lounge and put the television on full blast at three o'clock in the morning. Or, if he became agitated, he would thrash his arms around and kick. It wasn't uncommon for me to be hit across the head, or kicked in the shins. Call this living? You must be joking!

Ralph was so mischievous. He waited until I was out of the house for a few hours to get up to his most sensational tricks – like deciding that the kitchen ceiling tiles could do with a paint, climb up, lift them down one by one, numbering them because he knew he wouldn't remember how to put them back. Then he rigged up a trestle table with paint pots and brushes leaning against the microwave, and started to paint. On my return I found my newly-cleaned kitchen awash with loft insulation fibres, fluttering down from the ceiling above onto the kitchen table and floor, and every work surface. It was a war zone all right, I was absolutely furious and Ralph was so exhausted from his efforts that he was totally zonked out in the chair, oblivious of the fact that I had even entered the house. When I asked why he did this he said it was because I wouldn't let him climb. My reason was that if he overbalanced and felt dizzy I was terrified he would fall and hit his head.

Living with Parkinson's is a nightmare. One that you long to wake up from, but sadly don't. Every day is a crisis: falls, cut head, hospitalization, stitches and emergency care. All the time you have to try to be forgiving and begin again, but it's not easy. I class myself as a reasonably patient person, but Parkinson's disease, and Ralph's anger concerning it, took me to the brink. I punched my kitchen and bathroom walls in sheer frustration, screaming because he wouldn't cooperate with me over taking his tablets.

'Why are you winding yourself up?' Ralph would say. 'I'm not doing anything. You're doing it to yourself!'

And do you know, he was right. I was doing it to myself, but I couldn't stop. He drove me to total distraction because I never had a moment's mental peace. How I longed to go to sleep and not wake up. I really didn't care whether I lived or died.

A thought

There will be many people who find themselves in a caring role, not because they chose it, but because it was thrust upon them. People are caring for loved ones with mental illness and mental health issues, or physical conditions that affect brain functioning. The person they knew and loved is now like a dependent child. It's so hard to focus on the fact that those whose behaviour is so adverse were once a loving, responsible partner. All the time, one finds oneself saying, 'It's the illness, they can't help it.' Yet, at the back of our mind there's that little voice that says, 'I wonder if they know what they're doing?' True to say, sometimes they do!

A prayer

Lord, for all those who are drained by their responsibility, give them strength. Give them a patient demeanour when they feel like screaming. When it all gets too much, help them to walk away. Give them the strength to go on, help them to find an oasis of calm in sharing their dilemma with you. As their loved one gets further and further from them, help them to cope

32

A trip that would make a difference

———•◦•———

Throughout all our struggle, the work of The Lin Berwick Trust continued. We had our first cottage in East Harling, Norfolk. We were then looking for a second site. Where it would come from, I had no idea. I knew we just had to go forward in faith. It was decided that we should aim for our next property to be in the north. The way forward was to have a high-profile fundraising event. This was to be sponsored by The Ford Motor Company, and took the form of a fundraising dinner on the Royal Yacht *Britannia* with ninety-six guests.

Principal guests were to be the then Duke and Duchess of Hamilton, later known to us as Angus and Kay. Plans were going ahead swimmingly for this great occasion. The trustees had asked whether it would be possible for Ralph and I to attend, and although Ralph was extremely nervous, he agreed that we would go. However, we would need to take a carer to assist with the driving and caring for me, as Ralph now found this task more and more difficult. True to form, on the evening before the event, Ralph suddenly announced that he wasn't going. Nothing would induce him to motivate himself.

'Okay, I'll go with a carer by myself,' I exclaimed in sheer desperation, 'and we'll have a good time together.'
'You wouldn't dare!' was Ralph's surprised response. 'You couldn't possibly manage without me.'
'I could,' I answered. 'And I will.'

This motivated Ralph sufficiently to start cramming his clothes into a suitcase, including his dinner jacket, dress shirt and bow tie. By the time we had gone through all this procedure it was close on midnight. I sat on my bed, totally exhausted, in floods of tears.

'Lord, if we're to get to Scotland,' I asked, 'then make our efforts count.'

It was a truly wonderful weekend, exploring Leith and discovering the development of the Dockland area. We stumbled across a wonderful Mexican restaurant, which I enjoyed greatly. The occasion on the Royal Yacht *Britannia* was stunning. It was the first time I had ever worn a full-length evening gown, and it was gorgeous. Sitting on either side of me were Kay and Angus. I was terrified, yet I need not have worried. Kay was particularly charming, putting me at my ease. Formerly, she had been a Macmillan nurse, so was understanding of any difficulties I might have. We instantly gelled and there was a mutual admiration between us.

After dinner, I made a speech about our work, and the fact that we were looking for a second plot. The evening was a great success. The following day, I had a call from Angus. He and Kay had been talking about how they could help me and the Trust. They had wandered around the Hamilton Estate and found a clearing in the woodland, which they thought would be a good place for a holiday cottage. They requested that Ralph and I visit their estate at Dirleton, in East Lothian, to see if the area that they had earmarked was suitable.

We arrived on a cold December day and went into the woodland. Among the trees, the air was clean and crisp, wonderfully fresh. Apart from the odd twittering of birds, it was still and peaceful. It would be heavenly.

We were subsequently offered a plot of land for a peppercorn rent, on a ninety-nine-year lease, to build a holiday home for people with disability, their families and carers. Denis Duncan House, as it was to be called (named after our vice president, The Reverend Dr Denis Duncan, a former Church of Scotland minister) was opened in April 2006. A wonderful achievement for the Trust. And for our triumph over adversity.

A thought

Sometimes we have to go through a testing time to discover what good can come out of it. When we ask God to make something really count, he usually does, because we have gone forward in faith, not knowing what the answer will be, but trusting. It's so difficult to trust when you can't tell which way the arrow is pointing on your own particular crossroads. If I had given in, and said, 'Okay, we're not flying to Scotland', probably Denis Duncan House would never have been built. It is a salutary lesson that when one wants to achieve something that is so important, it's necessary to push the boundaries.

A prayer

Lord, when our shout to you for help is truly genuine, please answer it. When we don't know which way to turn, give us direction. When we are afraid of the task that we must perform to reach our goal, give us courage. Help us to find the right people along life's way, to encourage us, build us up and help us to grow. To grow in confidence is a wonderful revelation. To experience trust and open-heartedness is also a great privilege.

Lord, we thank you for those people who come into our lives as an unknown quantity, yet are special, and come to hold a place in our hearts that is second to none. Lord, help us to find the right people in the right place, and be thankful for them.

33

Personal cost

The success of our second holiday home was at a personal cost. Ralph became increasingly anxious, never wanting to socialize. My home was becoming more and more of a prison, as I hardly went outside the door. I tried to motivate Ralph, but to no avail. All he was interested in was the television. Mindlessly sitting in front of it for hours on end. It was usually on from three in the morning until well past midnight. If it had not been for BBC Radio 4, which kept me sane, I don't know what I would have done. It was my salvation to have stimulating, thought-provoking talks, rather than violence depicted on the screen for its own sake.

Ralph was becoming more and more depressed and taking increased antidepressants, which were not solving his problems but making them worse, causing him to hallucinate. It was quite fascinating to hear him describe what he could see. Ladies in crinoline dresses with big bustles, and little old men in breeches, standing in our hallway. They were so real that Ralph would go up to where he thought the figures were and try to touch them. Of course, his hand went right through because what he could see wasn't there. This was quite a scary time. In fact, it was downright terrifying, and extremely frustrating, because I could do nothing to pacify him when he behaved in this way.

I was getting out of my depth, feeling in total despair of my situation, helpless to do anything tangible for Ralph. The medics didn't seem to care. I was coping with all of this as a blind person, predominantly on my own. Ralph's mind may have been in a fog of confusion; mine was in a total panic, wondering what I would have to face next.

Where was God in all of this? I truly didn't know.

A thought

When long-term illness suddenly becomes more progressive, it's a terrifying experience for the onlookers. Those who are suffering are also confused, although they may not truly know the extent of their deterioration. Sometimes it can be a heart-stopping moment that makes you step back and look at what is going on. It's hard to summon up the strength to go forward. Every step forward feels as if the never-ending nightmare just keeps marching on. If we know someone who is experiencing such a time, then we should be there for them, supporting them in whatever way possible. This kind of illness is not something that we should walk away from. Rather, it's something to face head on and meet the challenge.

A prayer

Lord, when we face this type of challenge in our everyday existence, be there for us. Give us the patience, the strength, the ingenuity, to tackle every new situation. Help us to be brave. Help us to face life with dignity. Still keeping a sense of purpose. Help us not to shut ourselves away from the world as though we were ashamed. But help us, Lord, to be 'matter-of-fact' about what's happening, not sweeping the issues under the carpet, but facing them. Help us to create greater understanding of progressive illness and mental health. De-stigmatizing what it means, treating it as though it were any other illness, rather than something to be ashamed of. Help us to support the person who is struggling, who feels confused by what's happening to them. Not in a patronizing way, but in a way that helps them keep their identity.

34

A painful parting

Ralph's deterioration, both mentally and physically, took a huge downturn. He was constantly falling, finding himself in a totally agitated state, unable to stand. After two falls in the middle of the night, which my carer and I had to cope with, it was time to call the doctor. Ralph was taken into hospital, where he stayed for seventeen and a half weeks.

Travelling the thirty-mile round trip, six days a week, for seventeen and a half weeks, brought me to my knees, both emotionally and physically. I was absolutely shattered. Visiting Ralph was no joy. He was exceedingly angry with me for putting him into the hospital. He saw it as total rejection. Ralph went into non-cooperation mode and played up like a child, ignoring the doctors and generally being totally disruptive. Doctors diagnosed Lewy Body disease. I said I didn't think the problem was his mental state, rather that he was angry and wanted to cause maximum disruption.

When Ralph realized that the staff at the hospital were writing down everything that he did, this absurd behaviour stopped. Sadly, the spell in hospital rendered him unable to walk and non-weight bearing. He also had many other medical issues. Due to my physical limitations, I felt that the only way to deal with our situation was for Ralph to go into care. This was the start of the most devastating period of my life. I felt so incredibly guilty and, if I'm honest, I still do. Yet, I knew that it was a total impossibility for me to care for Ralph adequately, given the limitations of our house and its various facilities, and all the emotional disruption of Ralph's condition.

There were many case conferences, and many obstacles to overcome. It was a period in my life when I felt utterly bereft and utterly alone. It was worse than a bereavement, because the person I loved was still there. It's not until you find yourself in this difficult situation that you can ever truly understand the emotional trauma that the carer, or loved one, goes through. It's as though it were a sense of betrayal, especially as I was remaining in the family home, and was out in the community, seemingly doing all the things that I wanted to do. The reality was anything but this. I was in such a state of shock that I was functioning on auto-pilot, barely going through the motions of living. As for a social life, it was almost non-existent. Sometimes I didn't leave the house for sixteen weeks at a time, other than to visit Ralph.

Finding the most suitable care home is a traumatic experience. If I'm honest, no care home, however good, would be good enough for the person that I love. Social services, local authorities and medical staff were not particularly helpful at this stage. They seemed to have no concept of the difficulty that my blindness caused me. They just presented me with sheaf after sheaf of papers, none of which I could read. This was on the one hand insulting, and on the other completely thoughtless.

Daily life was a battleground, with little emotional and physical strength to do all the tasks that I had to do. More importantly, I didn't have the will. If someone had said to me at this time in my life that I only had six months to live, I would have welcomed it. I didn't want to get up in the morning. The thought of another day was just too terrible to contemplate. I longed for the night-time and for sleep to come, but sadly it didn't. I spent hours worrying and being awake.

A thought

When something happens that we have no real choice over, it is desperately hard to come to terms with the guilt that we feel.

Placing a loved one into a care home feels as though you are consigning them to a prison sentence. However wonderful the care home might be. Residential care and profound disability takes away freedom of choice and independence. It's incredibly difficult to find a level of motivation, on both sides.

The guilt that one experiences never goes away. Whatever one does to minimize a feeling of loss, it can never compensate. Where does the person in the care home vent their anger? It's usually on the person that put them there. Thus compounding the hurt feelings that are already present.

A prayer

Lord, when we have to make life-changing, momentous decisions, give us strength, peace of mind, serenity of spirit. Help us not to feel the burden of terrible guilt. But to find a middle ground where we can be strong enough to take the anger and walk away from it intact. Help us to hold onto the love that we shared between us, even in the most difficult times. Help us to always tell each other how much we care. Help us, Lord, to still find the person we loved through the quagmire of emotional suffering, and be thankful that we are still together, despite it all.

35

The peace of acceptance

————•◦•————

Four years on life had taken on a more peaceful turn. Ralph was not kicking quite so hard. There was more a sense of resignation and acceptance of his situation. Life had more or less returned to normal, whatever that might mean. I was picking up the pieces of my life: writing again, lecturing and doing disability consultancy work. All this helped me to keep the house afloat in terms of paying the bills and general maintenance, although Ralph, bless his heart, still helped me in this regard. Without some support from him, I would have been incredibly hard-pressed to manage.

I now had live-in care and was managing within the community. In addition, I had a wheelchair-accessible vehicle, partly funded by Access to Work, which I used for my lecturing and other work. This also enabled me to get Ralph home on a regular basis, where he spent time and we had an element of sharing.

Ralph had severe problems with his Parkinson's disease, and was now a permanent wheelchair user, barely able to feed himself. His speech was very difficult to understand, particularly in my case because I wasn't able to look at him, and therefore didn't get the facial clues. His communication was always worse when he had an infection. Infections seemed to come thick and fast. We went from crisis to crisis, and I never knew when I was going to receive a call telling me that Ralph had to go into hospital. But we lived one day at a time. Sometimes just five minutes at a time.

Visits from friends were very important. Certain friends visited Ralph on a regular basis. His daughter visited him weekly and this gave him great joy. Sadly, his son wasn't able to come to terms with his father's disability and didn't visit. This caused Ralph great sadness and feelings of rejection.

As for our relationship, when we were not together we talked regularly, sometimes up to five times a day, on the telephone. These conversations had to be short due to the fact that it was difficult for Ralph to hold the telephone and dial the numbers. He found it easier to communicate by using the receiver, rather than the hands-free facility, which amplified his already difficult speech. Ralph now had a very pleasant room in the home, with a patio garden that friends helped him create. He loved the antics of the squirrels and watching the birds going in and out of the nesting boxes. Nature had become tremendously important to him. He loved looking at the changing seasons and appreciating their beauty. More importantly, he enjoyed sharing what he saw with me, describing it to me.

Ralph sat in a very high chair, which meant that I couldn't reach him from mine to give him a hug, and this made me feel desolate. I would love to have been able to take him in my arms and give him a hug, and let him know that everything would be all right.

We didn't know what lay ahead. We could only live for the present, and make the most of whatever God-given time we had. One thing is for certain, we never missed an opportunity to tell each other how we felt and how we cared for one another. That was a tremendous privilege. Some people never get the chance.

A thought

When life deals us a very cruel blow it's hard to see the good in it. It's even harder to appreciate the world and its beauty in small things. We spend our time worrying about the big issues in life, when really it's the little issues that make the world go around. It's important that we never lose sight of tiny values and how we can express our love in so many different ways.

Love is not just sexual. Love is about respecting and valuing, and honouring the person that you care for.

A prayer

Lord, sometimes it's hard to find you in the small things. When life seems so bleak we are often blinded to the world around us. Grief and sadness cuts us off from beauty, because we feel submerged by what we are dealing with. Help us to reach out and be touched by small elements of beauty, kindness from one another, a welcome letter, a prayer or a visit from someone that we love.

Help us never to turn people away when the telephone call or the visit is inconvenient. For if we do this, we know that sooner or later they will stop coming. Help us not to be cut off by our tragedy and grief, but to move forward and reach out towards the light.

36

My best friend

It was Princess Diana who famously once said, 'There were three of us in this marriage.' In our case there certainly were – namely, Ralph, myself and Harvey, our chocolate English Cocker Spaniel. He came into our life when he was eleven weeks old. Ralph and I had always been dog lovers and wanted our life to be complete by having a dog as part of our family. But I had worried as to whether it would be fair because of looking after it.

Doctors recommended that I had a pet to help me ease my stress and pain levels. The chance of owning Harvey came up. His owner had to put him into a kennel because she found she was allergic to his fur. Harvey came to us on a ten-day trial basis, and has now been with me for six and a half years. He's the most gentle, soft, beautiful creature I have ever known.

When he came he was this little bundle of joy, all feet and ears, snuggling up to us for warmth and comfort. He slept under the seat of my wheelchair for security. When Ralph reached the point of not being able to walk him, a walker from the Cinnamon Trust stepped in. Viv became part of our family, and loves Harvey as though he were her own. Viv has done a wonderful job walking him almost three miles a day on a near-daily basis. My carers and other friends step in when she isn't available.

Harvey hasn't suffered because he's had disabled owners. Rather, he's been enriched by them. The love he shows is incredible. I tell him to guide me around the house. He runs in front squeaking his noisiest toy to tell me where he is. When his daddy visited, he climbed up onto the table top of Ralph's wheelchair and acted as my advocate, getting as close to him as he possibly could. Harvey went absolutely mad, licking Ralph furiously and climbing onto his chest. Ralph never failed to be moved by this display of excitement, from this wonderful dog that he thought would forget him. There's no chance that Harvey would ever forget Ralph. We were a complete family when we were together. When Ralph was home Harvey sat between us and watched his daddy intently. He whined at the front door when Ralph left the house, and then came back to me for a cuddle.

Harvey is my 'cuddles', my close companionship now. And it's wonderful how an animal can break down tension and barriers that humans so often put up. I love stroking his beautiful face, feeling those long ears that almost tuck under his chin. The curls on the top of his head, and the shape of his head, remind me of a learned judge. I love Harvey to bits.

A thought

We never can truly imagine the healing qualities that the love of an animal can give to us. Their love is unconditional. That's what makes it so special. Human love is always conditional. An animal is never afraid to give you affection, letting you know quite clearly how they feel. Humans so often hold back, feeling self-conscious, and restrain from telling people that they love them. A dog or a cat makes it abundantly clear that they care. Animals don't have such strong mood swings, but seemingly will always be the same. They reward all the things that we do for them with this unfailing warmth, which is truly wonderful.

A prayer

Lord, we thank you for the joy that having a pet can bring. We thank you that it can reach us in time of low spirits. Our pets can be personal confidants: talking to them and knowing that what we tell them won't go anywhere else is a precious gift.

Lord, we thank you for the affection that an animal can give to a human being. Animals reach out and touch where others fail. We thank you for guide dogs, for hearing dogs and pets for therapy, who do such wonderful work. We thank you for organizations, such as The Cinnamon Trust, who walk the animals when their owners can't, enabling the owner to feel that they have done right by their pet. Owning a pet is a responsibility, but a very precious one. Thank you, Lord, for your loving creatures that mean so much to so many.

37

The final walk

In my last meditation I spoke of the unity within my family: Ralph, myself and Harvey, our dog, who meant so much to Ralph. Ralph had had a very difficult year, with lots of bouts of infection and trips to hospital, becoming more and more fatigued and weakened by the whole process.

Ralph told me he was tired of life. When his speech really failed I knew that the end was near. I watched – feeling desperate, desolate, helpless and hopeless. Where had the hope gone? What was God trying to say to us? We had walked the walk of progressive, long-term illness together, and mutually carried the cross. Every piece of indignity that the illness gave to Ralph I felt too. Every time he was a step further down the terminal road, I bore it with him. And it was our own personal crucifixion.

Ralph was a deeply courageous man, finally making the decision that he had endured enough, and empowering himself in the only way he knew how, which was to refuse medication, water and food. This was a huge step to take. One, if I am honest, I do not know if I would have had the courage to make.

Ralph asked to see Harvey, who climbed all over him and he clung onto Harvey that day in a way that he had never done before. On reflection, I know he was saying goodbye. The end, for Ralph, took some twelve days, and I was at his bedside, feeling and listening to this process (because I have no sight). It was a truly unforgettable experience, and yet, in many ways, it was an experience that was a very great privilege. Desolating though the end was, I had an enormous sense of Ralph's struggle being over. I am grieving, of course, but if all I grieved for was for this man to remain, I would be totally selfish. How could I wish him to endure the suffering that he was experiencing? It would not have been an expression of my love for him, to wish him to remain.

I know that when I grieve I am not grieving for Ralph. For he is free. I am grieving, selfishly, for myself. Long-term illness is a hard road to travel. Every step of it is like Christ carrying his cross to Calvary and falling to his knees along the way, because he could not bear the burden upon his back. The onlookers were as helpless as Christ that day. When I think of my husband's situation, in the end I was as helpless as he.

A thought

When someone you love, or someone you are very close to, is diagnosed with a long-term, progressive illness, it is hard to stay the course with them. So many so-called friends fall by the wayside, because to visit someone with long-term illness on a regular basis takes commitment and it is time consuming. It is also incredibly hard to watch the person you knew literally change before your eyes, somehow become a different person due to illness. In reality they are no different. They are still the person we once loved. There you are, you see, I am as guilty as the next person, because in what I have just written, I have used the past tense. Not deliberately, but it happens because we have a different mindset towards the person we cared about. Why should this be? They are still the person we knew and loved. Just because their physical body alters, it does not mean that they change. There are times when it is so hard to hold onto that fact, because possibly your loved one is experiencing confusion, or hallucinating, or just being generally very unwell.

Yet, all the time we have to hold on to the precious memories; the things that we loved about them and were attracted to them for, either in love or friendship. It is a difficult concept, but it can be done. We must help the person who is ill to not think of themselves as a 'non-person' because their life has changed. After all, if we demean them to that extent, then we are only demeaning ourselves still further.

A prayer

Lord, when we are faced with knowing that our loved one has a long-term illness, it is terrifying. Help us to be able to be strengthened to walk the long, arduous journey with them. Give us the courage to strengthen that person facing long-term illness, and be there for them. Good days and bad. Regardless of what it does to us.

Help us to realize that although long-term illness can be crucifying to all those concerned, the release through death can be their resurrection, their victory over suffering. Help us to be glad that their suffering is over, and know that you will be there with those who remain.